Finding My Way

A Path from Stagnation to Divine Acceleration

Cathy L. Benson

ISBN: 9798340489982

DEDICATION

This dedication is to those who have faced the shadows of stagnation, where progress seemed distant, and dreams felt deferred. To those who, despite the weight of uncertainty and the whispers of doubt, chose to rise above, pushing through barriers with unwavering determination. Your journey from stillness to movement, from hesitation to action, is a testament to the power of resilience and the unyielding spirit within. You remind us of all that even in the quietest moments, growth is taking place, preparing us for the acceleration to come.

To those who have not only overcome but have thrived, entering a season of divine acceleration, this is for you. You have embraced the winds of change, allowing them to carry you to heights once unimaginable. Your courage, faith, and perseverance have turned obstacles into steppingstones, and what once held you back now propels you forward with divine purpose. May your journey inspire others to trust in their process, knowing that with patience and persistence, they too can experience the boundless momentum that comes with divine acceleration.

Lastly, I dedicate this book to my late mother, Mary Catherine Benson, and my late aunt, Betty Ruth Adams. I know I have made them proud.

ACKNOWLEDGEMENTS

First giving honor to God Almighty from whom all blessings flow, I am extremely honored and grateful for this moment. To my beautiful daughters, I am truly nothing without you. Aasia thank you for being my strong tower, my voice of reason, and Zion Faith, thank you for being my strength and my motivation. To my daddy and my family thank you for everything I love you each of you.

To my wonderful village, my baby sister Dionne Slaton, my Duchess, words cannot express what you mean to me, you have been with me through some of my toughest storms and I thank you. Venetia A. Daley, my (JS) I cannot begin to thank God enough for placing you in my path because you are my eyes when I cannot see and my voice when I am unable to formulate words to express how I feel, lastly you have been my counselor and my prayer warrior. Christina Gammage, the one who would not let me stop no matter what was placed in my path, and the one who shared the journey of pain with me. Dinane Foster and Lanise Linson my heartbeats, you all saw the vision before I could write it. Each of you saw my true potential and the many things that I would accomplish in the physical realm and I thank you.

It's impossible to speak of the beautiful women without mentioning the giants who stood by me during this entire process. Bryan White, thank you for seeing the true me and for listening when I needed it the most, but most of all thanks for all the love you have given me and all the wonderful ideas that made this project possible. Johnny Barlow, a huge God Bless You for being there holding my hand, pushing me the hardest when I desperately wanted to give up but most of all being who you are in my life. Chuck Nobles, you saw the vision at such the age of 12 years old and you, my brother, prayed for this moment and I am thankful that you have received the chance to witness it firsthand. Lonte Butler, my oldest and dearest friend, thank you for supporting the vision and the dream within me. P.K. thank you for the journey, but most of all thank you for being a friend who never gave up on me. Apostle Bobby E. Stapleton, Jr. the man who saw the vision before I saw the potential within me. Apostle, you were the first to allow me to fulfill my dream and to truly walk in it which led me to this moment. I thank you for your leadership as well as your friendship, you know what you have done to make this moment possible, and may God give it back to you one hundredfold.

Last, but not least, I would not be the writer I am today, and this moment would not be possible if it wasn't for the two women who saw the pain and hurt that was within me and provided me with an outlet to soar and to release, but most of all that led me to the path of healing. Thank You, Ms. Maronda Parker, and Mrs. Sharetta Donalson. Maronda, Twenty-Five Speak became my outlet and it became a vital instrument in my healing journey. Sharetta, in my darkest hour and most painful moment you looked beyond my flaws, and you saw a young woman crying for help and because of you I am now stronger, wiser, and healed. I take nothing away from this moment because I am no longer stagnant for, I have accelerated to my divine purpose in life.

CONTENTS

Foreword

When I first met Cathy, I knew there was something uniquely powerful about her—an authenticity and depth that couldn't help but shine through. Over the years, I have had the privilege of watching her navigate life's twists and turns, with both courage and vulnerability. Her journey has been one of discovery—of herself, of her purpose, and of the meaning of life's most profound moments.

"Finding My Way" is not just a book; it's a reflection of Cathy's soul, capturing the rawness of her struggles, the beauty of her triumphs, and the wisdom she's gathered along the way. It's a story of resilience, transformation, and ultimately, hope. Through these pages, you'll not only get a glimpse into her life but also see parts of your own journey mirrored back to you.

I am honored to write this foreword and even more honored to call Cathy (Sunshine) my friend. Her words have touched my heart in ways I can't fully describe, and I know they will do the same for you. So, as you embark on this reading experience, prepare to be moved, challenged, and inspired to find your own way, just as she has so beautifully done.

Cathy, no one deserves the amount of attention, worthiness, or honor this book will garner more than you. I am so proud of you!! May God bless your hands and your heart to continue to push His kingdom!

With love and admiration always,

Lonte Butler

Preface

Finding my way is a book filled with hurt, pain, sadness, joy, triumphant, and success. I have taken the topics of my life and compiled them within the pages of this book. I was once a young woman stuck and living in the past filled with uncertainty but filled with stagnation. I was comfortable with knowing that this is where my life will end. I became fearful of what life could truly bring. I felt lonely and unworthy as well as unwanted. Often crying to God asking him for help yet I failed to help myself. It was the day I sat before my mother's casket reflecting of all the things that happened to me in life that I didn't get a chance to tell her or the moment I sat in the therapist office filled with rage and resentment. I hated the individuals who hurt me, but I hated myself more for putting up with it. Through therapy and finding my way back to God I was able to find my true self and my true divine purpose in life. Although, I was stagnant and comfortable with the known I became excited about the unknown because I began to trust God.

My ultimate goal for this book is that my story will resonate within the pit of your soul, and you will learn to trust God even when you don't understand, trust God although you can't trace him, trust him even when he is silent, but most importantly learn to trust yourself. I want you to understand it's ok to come out of your place of comfort and explore the life of wonderful things that God has given unto you. Many failures are from the many opportunities that we don't take. So, journey with me through the topics of how I went from bitterness, betrayal, unforgiveness, hurt, pain, and stagnation to divine acceleration by accepting who I was and whose I was. I welcome you to: "Finding My Way: A Path from Stagnation to Divine Acceleration."

Introduction

Accelerating spiritually is essential because it propels us toward deeper understanding, connection, and purpose in our lives. Spiritual growth encourages us to move beyond complacency and routine, pushing us to explore the vast potential within us. By continually seeking to grow, we align ourselves with higher truths and wisdom, allowing us to live more authentically and compassionately. Stagnation, on the other hand, keeps us anchored in old patterns, preventing us from experiencing the fullness of life and the profound peace that comes with spiritual advancement. In a world where change is constant, spiritual acceleration equips us to navigate challenges with grace and resilience. It fosters a sense of inner strength and clarity, enabling us to respond to life's uncertainties with faith and purpose. When we accelerate spiritually, we open ourselves to greater love, wisdom, and understanding, which not only enriches our own lives but also positively impacts those around us.

Chapter One
Fear & Without Direction

Life's journey is marked by a series of choices and uncertainties that shape our path. For many, faith provides a guiding light, offering direction and solace. However, when one walks through life without such a divine compass, the journey can be fraught with fear and confusion. This chapter explores the experience of navigating life without a sense of direction from God, examining the psychological and existential impacts, as well as potential pathways to finding meaning and purpose.

Walking through life without a perceived divine direction often leads to heightened anxiety and fear. Without the assurance of a higher power guiding one's steps, individuals may struggle with a sense of aimlessness. This lack of direction can manifest as existential dread, where the individual questions the meaning of their existence and their place in the world. Fear, in this context, can be both existential and practical. Existential fear arises from the uncertainty of one's purpose and the ultimate meaning of life. This can lead to a sense of emptiness and a pervasive anxiety about the future. Practical fears, on the other hand, relate to day-to-day decisions and the fear of making wrong choices without a divine blueprint to guide them.

Psychologically, the absence of a perceived divine direction can erode self-confidence. When individuals do not believe that their lives are part of a greater plan, they might struggle with self-doubt and a lack of motivation. This can result in a state of paralysis where fear of making mistakes prevents them from taking decisive action. The existential challenge of living without divine guidance touches on deeper philosophical questions about human purpose and meaning.

Despite the challenges of walking through life without divine direction, there are ways to find meaning and cope with fear. One approach is to cultivate a sense of purpose through personal goals and values. Setting meaningful objectives and pursuing passions can provide a sense of direction and fulfillment. Another strategy is to seek connections with others. Building relationships and engaging in community can provide support and a sense of belonging, which can alleviate feelings of isolation and fear. Human connections often offer comfort and perspective that can help navigate the uncertainties of life. Mindfulness and self-reflection can also be valuable tools. Practices like meditation and journaling can help individuals explore their thoughts and emotions, providing clarity and reducing anxiety. By becoming more attuned to their inner selves, individuals can gain insights into their values and aspirations, which can guide their decisions and actions. Additionally, exploring various philosophical and spiritual frameworks can offer new perspectives on life's challenges. While one may not subscribe to a particular religion, engaging with different belief systems and philosophies can provide valuable insights and tools for finding personal meaning.

Walking through life without a perceived divine direction presents significant challenges, including heightened fear and existential uncertainty. The psychological impacts can be profound, leading to anxiety and self-doubt. However, by embracing personal responsibility, setting meaningful goals, building connections, and exploring philosophical perspectives, individuals can navigate these challenges and find their sense of purpose and direction. Ultimately, while the absence of divine guidance can be daunting, it also opens the door to personal growth and self-discovery. By actively engaging in their journey, individuals can transform fear and uncertainty into opportunities for profound personal development and fulfillment

A Prayer During a time of Fear & Without Direction

Heavenly Father,

I come before You with a heart burdened by fear and uncertainty. In moments when I feel lost and without direction, I am overwhelmed by the weight of the unknown. I struggle to find my way and to understand the path You have set before me. Lord, I ask for Your comfort and peace, for only You can calm the storms within me and guide me through the darkness.

Father, I confess that my faith sometimes wavers, and I allow fear to take hold of my thoughts. I am uncertain of the future, and this lack of direction fills me with anxiety. But I know that You are a God of clarity and purpose and that You have a plan for my life. Please help me to trust in Your divine wisdom, even when I cannot see the way ahead. Strengthen my faith so that I may walk confidently in Your light.

Lord, I seek Your guidance in all that I do. I know that without You, I am like a ship without a sail, drifting aimlessly in the vast sea of life. I ask that You lead me, step by step, and grant me the courage to follow wherever You direct. Teach me to be still and listen for Your voice, and to find peace in the knowledge that You are always with me, even during confusion and doubt.

Finally, I thank You, God, for Your unfailing love and mercy. I am grateful that even in my moments of fear and uncertainty, you never leave me alone. You are my refuge and strength, a constant presence in times of trouble. Help me to remember that no matter how lost I may feel, I am always found in You. Guide my steps, Lord, and fill my heart with the assurance of Your perfect plan for my life.

In Jesus' name, I pray. Amen.

Chapter Two
Who is the Creator?

The concept of the Creator is central to many religious and philosophical traditions around the world. For billions of people, the Creator is understood as the ultimate source of all existence, the one who brought the universe and everything within it into being. In the Christian tradition, God is recognized as the Creator, and to be a follower of God is to align oneself with His will, to live according to His teachings, and to seek a relationship with Him. This chapter explores the identity of the Creator as understood in the Christian faith and examines what it means to be a true follower of God, delving into the spiritual, ethical, and communal aspects of this relationship. In the Christian tradition, the Creator is identified as God, the one who spoke the universe into existence. According to the Bible, particularly in the book of Genesis, God created the heavens and the earth, bringing forth light, life, and order from the chaos. He is depicted as omnipotent, omniscient, and omnipresent qualities that affirm His absolute sovereignty over all creation.

The very first verse of the Bible, "In the beginning, God created the heavens and the earth" (Genesis 1:1), sets the stage for understanding God as the ultimate source of everything that exists. God's role as Creator is not limited to the initial act of creation. He is also seen as the sustainer of the universe, actively involved in the ongoing existence and governance of all things. In Christian theology, this continuous involvement is a testament to God's love and care for His creation. Furthermore, God is not a distant or detached Creator; rather, He is deeply relational, seeking to establish a personal connection with human beings, who are made in His image. This relational aspect of God is crucial in understanding what it means to be a follower of God. In addition to being the Creator, God is also the moral lawgiver. He provides the moral framework within which His followers are to live. This framework is revealed through the Scriptures, particularly in the Ten Commandments and the teachings of Jesus Christ. God's moral law is an expression of His holy and righteous nature, and it serves as a guide for how His followers should conduct their lives. To follow God is to adhere to this moral code, not out of fear of punishment, but out of love and reverence for the Creator.

To be a follower of God is, first and foremost, a spiritual journey. This journey begins with recognizing God's sovereignty and acknowledging one's dependence on Him. In Christian faith, this often involves a moment of conversion, where an individual turns away from sin and towards God, accepting Jesus Christ as their Savior. This act of faith is seen as the beginning of a new life, one that is marked by a relationship with God that grows deeper over time. The spiritual life of a follower of God is characterized by prayer, worship, and the study of Scripture. Prayer is a way of communicating with God, expressing one's thoughts, concerns, and desires, and seeking His guidance and wisdom. Worship, both in communal settings and in personal devotion, is an expression of reverence and adoration for God. It is a way of acknowledging God's greatness and his central place in the believer's life.
Studying Scripture is another vital aspect of following God. The Bible is considered the inspired word of God, providing instruction, encouragement, and insight into God's character and will. Through Scripture, followers of God learn about His promises, His expectations, and His plan for humanity. The teachings of Jesus serve as a model for how believers are to live, emphasizing love, compassion, forgiveness, and humility.

The spiritual journey also involves transformation. As followers of God grow in their faith, they are gradually transformed into the likeness of Christ. This process, known as sanctification, is a work of the Holy Spirit, who empowers believers to overcome sin and to live lives that reflect God's holiness. It is a lifelong journey that requires commitment, perseverance, and a willingness to submit to God's will. Being a follower of God carries with it significant ethical and moral responsibilities. The moral teachings of the Bible provide a framework for how believers are to conduct their lives, not only in their personal behavior but also in their interactions with others. The Ten Commandments, for example, offer foundational principles such as honoring one's parents, refraining from murder, theft, and adultery, and keeping the Sabbath holy. These commandments are not merely rules to be followed; they are expressions of God's desire for a just and loving community.

Jesus' teachings further expand on these principles, emphasizing the importance of love and compassion. The Great Commandment, which instructs believers to love God with all their heart, soul, and mind, and to love their neighbors as themselves, is central to Christian ethics. This commandment underscores the relational nature of following God relationships with both God and others are to be characterized by love, which reflects God's nature. Social justice is another important aspect of following God. The Bible repeatedly calls for justice for the oppressed, care for the poor, and protection for the vulnerable. In following God, believers are called to work for justice and peace in their communities and the wider world. This involves not only personal acts of charity but also advocating for systemic change that aligns with God's vision of a just and equitable society.

Ethical living as a follower of God also involves integrity and honesty. The Bible teaches that truthfulness and integrity are essential qualities of a righteous life. Followers of God are called to live in a way that is consistent with their faith, showing integrity in their words and actions, and being honest in their dealings with others. This commitment to ethical living reflects the believer's desire to honor God and to live according to His will. While the spiritual journey is deeply personal, following God is also a communal experience. The Christian faith is not meant to be lived in isolation; rather, it is intended to be practiced within the context of a community of believers. The Church, as the body of Christ, plays a central role in the life of a follower of God. It is within the Church that believers gather for worship, receive teaching, and find support and encouragement from one another. The Church provides a space for communal worship, where believers come together to honor God, hear His word, and participate in the sacraments. This communal aspect of worship is a powerful reminder that following God is not just an individual endeavor but a collective one. The shared experiences of worship and fellowship help to strengthen the bonds between believers and to create a sense of belonging and unity within the community.

Moreover, the Church is a place of service. Followers of God are called to serve one another and to use their gifts and talents for the benefit of the community. This service can take many forms, from teaching and mentoring to providing for the needs of the poor and the sick. The Church also engages in mission work, spreading the message of the Gospel and extending God's love to people outside the faith community. In addition to serving within the Church, followers of God are called to be witnesses to their faith in the wider world. This involves living out their beliefs in their daily lives and sharing the message of God's love with others. The Great Commission, given by Jesus to His disciples, instructs believers to "go and make disciples of all nations" (Matthew 28:19), emphasizing the importance of evangelism and the global mission of the Church.

The Creator, as understood in the Christian faith, is the sovereign and loving God who brought the universe into being and who continues to sustain it. To be a follower of God is to enter a relationship with this Creator, to live according to His teachings, and to seek to reflect His character in one's life. This journey involves spiritual growth, ethical living, and active participation in a community of believers. It is a journey marked by both challenges and profound rewards, as followers of God experience the joy of knowing and serving the Creator and the fulfillment of living a life that is aligned with His will.

A Prayer for Accepting Christ

Heavenly Father,

I come before You with a heart open to Your love and truth. I acknowledge that I need Your grace, and I confess my desire to know Christ more deeply and personally in my life. Lord, I recognize that Jesus is the way, the truth, and the life, and I want to fully accept Him as my Savior. Please remove any doubts or fears that may hinder me from embracing this truth completely. Help me to see clearly who Jesus is and what He means for my life.

Lord Jesus, I accept You into my heart as my Lord and Savior. I believe in the sacrifice You made on the cross for my sins and in Your resurrection, which gives me the hope of eternal life. I surrender my life to You, trusting in Your perfect will and guidance. Lead me on the path of righteousness and help me to follow You with a faithful and obedient heart. I ask for the strength and courage to live out my faith in You daily.

Holy Spirit, I invite You to fill me with Your presence and to guide me in understanding the depth of Christ's love for me. Open my eyes to see how Jesus is working in my life and give me the wisdom to recognize His voice. I pray that You would mold my heart to be more like Christ, growing in love, compassion, and humility. Help me to stay rooted in the truth of who Jesus is and to live in a way that honors Him.

Father, I thank You for the gift of salvation through Your Son, Jesus Christ. I am grateful for the new life I have in Him and for the assurance that I am forever loved and accepted by You. As I walk this journey of faith, I ask that You continue to reveal more of Christ to me each day. May I grow in my knowledge and love of Him, and may my life reflect His grace and truth.

In Jesus' precious name, I pray. Amen.

Chapter Three
The Wrongful Encounter

How might a trauma survivor at any point respond when the aggravation of the past reemerges, and nothing appears to attempt to make it better? Instead of battling the aggravation or truly regretting having it, survivors can attempt to coordinate their energy into allowing the pain of aggravation to turn into an optional piece of life. Trauma is the consequence of an adverse occasion. It will happen when you feel genuinely or intellectually hurt by something that has occurred. Imagine walking through life broken and shattered, well that is how I felt when I arrived home from college. After a long semester, I never thought the one place where I felt safe would become a prison filled with bad memories. How could the one person I admired the most in life be the demon who tarnished my shine and destroyed my joy? This is where the journey to brokenness begins.

A nightmare waiting to happen, as I arrived home excited to see my family and friends. It has been one long semester I thought to myself. As I sat down on my friend's bed, I began to look over my life. As I pondered on my career and where my life was headed, I drifted off to sleep. While dreaming of one day running the world, I was awakened by an unknown man. He placed his hands over my mouth, tied my hands behind my head, pulled down my pants, and entered a place where he didn't belong. I wanted to scream but no words would come out. He whispered in my ear, "If you scream, I will kill you. If you tell anyone, I will kill you." As tears streamed down my face, I felt trapped in a world where I didn't belong. As he penetrated me over and over, the moans from his breath filled the air, as agony grew stronger and stronger upon my face. He released his semen all over me while calling me a useless being, I lay there crying and in pain. After all, I was seven months pregnant with my first child. Laying there frightened and alone, how could something like this happen to me? I thought God loved me; what God would allow this to happen to me? Did I do something wrong for God to punish me in this way? Is it because I am pregnant at such an early age?

As a child, my mother taught me that God would be with me until the end of time. Well, God, where are you? Why did you allow this to happen to me? I didn't understand at that moment why things happen to me, but I will later learn everything that was created to break me, became necessary to make me stronger. Surviving a rape encounter is a deeply traumatic experience that can have long-lasting effects on a person's emotional, psychological, and physical well-being. The impact of such an assault extends far beyond the immediate physical harm and involves complex layers of emotional distress, mental health struggles, and social repercussions.

The psychological impact of rape is profound and multifaceted. Survivors often grapple with a range of intense emotions, including fear, shame, guilt, and anger. The violation of trust and personal autonomy that comes with rape can lead to significant mental health issues such as post-traumatic stress disorder (PTSD), depression, and anxiety. Survivors may experience flashbacks, nightmares, hypervigilance, and emotional numbness. Additionally, self-blame is common; survivors might question their actions or believe they somehow contributed to the assault.

The trauma of rape can also disrupt one's sense of self and identity. Survivors might struggle with issues related to body image, self-worth, and sexual intimacy. The assault can lead to a pervasive feeling of being unsafe or unworthy, which can affect various aspects of life, including relationships, work, and daily functioning. The challenge of overcoming these psychological hurdles requires comprehensive and empathetic support. Building a support network is another crucial aspect of coping. Support from trusted friends, family members, or support groups can offer validation and understanding. Support groups allow survivors to connect with others who have faced similar experiences, providing a sense of community and shared experience. Such connections can be instrumental in reducing feelings of isolation and fostering a sense of solidarity.

Self-care practices also play a significant role in coping. Engaging in activities that promote physical and emotional well-being, such as exercise, healthy eating, and mindfulness, can aid in the healing process. Establishing routines that provide a sense of normalcy and stability can help survivors regain control over their lives and rebuild their sense of self. Recovery from a rape encounter is a deeply personal journey, and there is no single path to healing. However, certain strategies can facilitate the process. Reclaiming one's narrative and sense of agency is an important aspect of recovery. This might involve setting boundaries, making decisions about personal safety, and reasserting control over one's life and body.

Empowerment often comes from engaging in activities that reinforce self-worth and personal growth. Pursuing hobbies, setting, and achieving personal goals, and building new relationships can help survivors rebuild their confidence and sense of purpose. Additionally, involvement in advocacy and support work can provide a sense of agency and contribute to a broader societal change. Healing is also supported by ongoing self-care and personal development. It is important for survivors to continue seeking professional help as needed and to practice self-compassion. Building a life that reflects one's values and aspirations can contribute to a renewed sense of identity and fulfillment. By addressing the psychological impact, utilizing effective coping strategies, and engaging in recovery efforts, survivors can work towards reclaiming their lives and fostering resilience. Society needs to provide compassionate support and advocate for systemic changes that promote understanding and justice for survivors of sexual violence. Through these efforts, it helped me on my journey to healing and empowerment.

A Prayer for Healing

Divine Healer,

In this moment of quiet reflection, I come before You with a heart heavy from the weight of trauma. I acknowledge the pain that lingers and the wounds that remain, both seen and unseen. Lord, I ask for Your grace and mercy to envelop me as I seek healing and restoration from this deeply distressing experience. I lay before You the burdens that I carry—fear, sorrow, and confusion. You know the depth of my suffering, and I trust in Your understanding and compassion. Please ease the turmoil within me and bring peace to my troubled heart. Help me to release the shackles of anxiety and distress that cling to my spirit. Grant me solace in Your presence and the strength to face each day with hope and courage. I pray for Your healing touch to mend the wounds of my soul. May Your love flow through me, bringing relief to the pain that lingers. Guide me to sources of comfort and support that will aid in my recovery. Surround me with individuals who will uplift and encourage me and grant me the wisdom to seek the help I need. May Your healing power restore not just my body, but also my spirit and mind.

Illuminate the path before me as I navigate this journey of healing. When I feel lost in darkness or overwhelmed by doubt, be my guiding light. Help me to find clarity amidst the confusion and to trust in Your plan for my life. Remind me of Your promises of renewal and hope and give me the faith to believe in the possibility of a brighter future. In moments of fear and isolation, draw near to me with Your comforting presence. Let me feel Your embrace and know that I am never alone. Help me to surrender my pain to You and find solace in Your unwavering love. Teach me to embrace the process of healing, even when it is slow or difficult. Grant me patience with myself and the courage to face the emotions and memories that arise. As I move forward, help me to forgive myself and those who may have caused me harm. Release me from the chains of bitterness and resentment and fill my heart with Your peace and grace. Teach me to see the good in myself and others, and to extend compassion and understanding where there is hurt. Let forgiveness be a pathway to my healing and the restoration of my spirit.

I place my trust in Your promises of renewal and transformation. Help me to envision a future beyond this pain, one filled with purpose and joy. Inspire me to pursue activities and relationships that nurture my healing and growth. Fill my heart with hope and optimism, and let Your love be the foundation upon which I rebuild my life. Grant me moments of stillness and reflection where I can connect with You and find comfort. Help me to cultivate inner peace through prayer, meditation, and quiet contemplation. Let Your peace guard my heart and mind and help me to remain centered in Your presence amidst the challenges I face. I lift this prayer with a heart full of hope and trust in Your infinite love and wisdom. May Your healing grace be upon me, and may I find strength and renewal in Your presence. Guide me through this journey with Your gentle hand, and may Your light continue to shine upon me as I walk toward healing and wholeness. In Your Holy Name, Amen.

Chapter Four
Overcoming the Pain

Overcoming pain after a traumatic event is a complex and deeply personal journey. Pain, whether physical, emotional, or psychological, often lingers long after the initial trauma has passed. This statement explores the multifaceted nature of trauma, the impact it has on an individual's life, and the various approaches to overcoming the pain associated with it. By examining the psychological and emotional processes involved, as well as the strategies that can aid in recovery, this discussion aims to provide a comprehensive understanding of how I navigated the aftermath of trauma and found pathways to healing. Trauma is an overwhelming experience that can shatter an individual's sense of safety and stability. It often involves exposure to situations that threaten one's life, physical integrity, or mental well-being, leading to a profound sense of helplessness. Traumatic events can include, but are not limited to, physical or sexual assault, natural disasters, accidents, war, and the sudden loss of a loved one. The pain that follows such events is multifaceted, manifesting in various ways, including post-traumatic stress disorder (PTSD), anxiety, depression, and a range of physical symptoms.

One of the most challenging aspects of overcoming pain after trauma is the way it disrupts an individual's sense of identity and worldview. The experience of trauma can lead to a loss of trust in oneself, others, and the world at large. This loss of trust can create a sense of isolation, as individuals may feel that no one else can understand their pain. Additionally, the memory of the traumatic event can become intrusive, replaying in the mind like a broken record and making it difficult to move forward. Healing from trauma is not a linear process; it is a journey that involves navigating a range of emotions and psychological states. Immediately following a traumatic event, individuals may experience shock, denial, and numbness as their mind tries to protect them from the full impact of what has occurred. As these initial defenses begin to fade, the pain of the trauma often surfaces, leading to feelings of grief, anger, sadness, and fear.

One of the key challenges in overcoming pain is learning to process and integrate these emotions rather than avoiding or suppressing them.

Suppression can lead to a buildup of unresolved pain, which may manifest in unhealthy ways, such as substance abuse, self-harm, or dissociation. Conversely, processing these emotions involves acknowledging and confronting the pain, allowing oneself to fully experience it, and eventually finding ways to make sense of it within the context of one's life. One such strategy is cultivating mindfulness and self-compassion. Mindfulness involves staying present and fully engaged in the moment, which can help individuals to manage anxiety and reduce the impact of intrusive memories. Self-compassion, on the other hand, involves treating oneself with the same kindness and understanding that one would offer to a friend in distress. By practicing self-compassion, individuals can begin to counteract the self-blame and harsh judgment that often accompany trauma.

Another important strategy is rebuilding a sense of safety and stability in one's life. Trauma can erode an individual's sense of security, making it difficult to feel safe in the world. Re-establishing routines, creating a supportive environment, and setting boundaries are all ways to rebuild a sense of safety. Additionally, engaging in activities that promote relaxation and well-being, such as exercise, meditation, or creative expression, can help to reduce stress and promote healing. One of the most profound aspects of overcoming pain after a traumatic event is the potential for post-traumatic growth. This concept refers to the positive psychological changes that can occur because of struggling with trauma. While not everyone who experiences trauma will necessarily undergo post-traumatic growth, for many, the process of overcoming pain can lead to a deeper understanding of themselves and the world around them.

Finding meaning in the aftermath of trauma is a key component of post-traumatic growth. This may involve re-evaluating one's values, priorities, and life goals, and making changes that align with a new sense of purpose. For some, the experience of trauma may lead to greater empathy and compassion for others, as well as a renewed appreciation for life. Others may find strength in their ability to overcome adversity and a sense of empowerment in having survived the trauma. It is important to note that finding meaning in trauma does not negate the pain or diminish the impact of the event. Rather, it is about finding a way to integrate the experience into one's life in a way that allows for growth and healing. This process may take time, and it is essential for individuals to be patient with themselves as they navigate their unique journey of recovery. Overcoming pain after a traumatic event is a deeply personal and multifaceted process. It involves not only addressing the emotional and psychological impact of the trauma but also finding ways to rebuild a sense of safety, stability, and connection in one's life. Through therapy, mindfulness, self-compassion, and social support, individuals can begin to process and integrate their pain, ultimately finding pathways to healing and growth. While the journey may be challenging, it is also an opportunity for profound transformation and the discovery of inner strength. By embracing the process of healing, individuals can reclaim their lives and move forward with a renewed sense of purpose and resilience.

A Prayer for Pushing Through the Pain

Heavenly Father,

In this moment of deep pain, I come before You with a heart that is heavy, a spirit that is weary, and a mind that is overwhelmed. I find myself burdened by the weight of suffering, and I feel as though I am drowning in the depths of despair. Yet, even during my struggle, I know that You are with me. You have promised never to leave me nor forsake me, and so I turn to You now, seeking Your strength, Your comfort, and Your guidance. Lord, I acknowledge that pain is a part of life, and that in this world, I will face trials and tribulations. Yet, I confess that there are times when the pain feels too much to bear, when I am tempted to give in to despair and hopelessness. But, Father, I know that You are greater than any pain I may endure, and I believe that You can help me push through this season of suffering.

Father, grant me the strength to endure. You are my Rock and my Fortress, and in You, I find refuge. When I am weak, you are strong. When I am weary, you are my rest. I pray that You will fill me with Your strength, that I may stand firm in the face of adversity. Help me to remember that I can do all things through Christ who strengthens me, and that Your power is made perfect in my weakness. When I feel like giving up, remind me of Your faithfulness, and help me to press on, knowing that You are with me every step of the way. Lord, I ask for Your comfort during my pain. You are the God of all comfort, who comforts us in all our afflictions. I pray that You will wrap Your loving arms around me, that I may feel Your presence and Your peace. When the pain feels overwhelming, I ask that You calm my troubled heart and quiet my anxious thoughts. Remind me that You are near, that You see my suffering, and that You care deeply for me. Help me to trust in Your unfailing love, and to find solace in the knowledge that You are my Good Shepherd, who leads me beside still waters and restores my soul.

Father, give me the courage to face my pain with faith. It is so easy to be consumed by fear and doubt when I am suffering. But I know that You have not given me a spirit of fear, but of power, love, and a sound mind. I pray that You will give me the courage to face my pain head-on, knowing that You are with me. Help me to trust in Your plan for my life, even when I cannot see the way forward. Remind me that You work all things together for good for those who love You and are called according to Your purpose. Give me the faith to believe that You can bring beauty out of my pain, and that You can use my suffering for Your glory. Lord, I ask for Your wisdom and guidance as I navigate this season of pain. I confess that I do not always know how to cope with my suffering, and that I often feel lost and confused. But I know that You are the source of all wisdom, and that You have promised to give wisdom generously to all who ask. I pray that You will guide my steps and lead me in the path that You have prepared for me. Help me to discern Your will for my life, and to make decisions that honor You. When I am tempted to take shortcuts or to seek relief in unhealthy ways, give me the wisdom to choose the path of righteousness and the strength to stay the course.

Father, I pray for the healing of my heart, mind, and body. You are the Great Physician, who heals all our diseases and binds up our wounds. I pray that You would bring healing to every part of me that is broken, that You would mend the shattered pieces of my heart, and that You would restore me to wholeness. I know that healing may not always come in the way or the timing that I desire, but I trust that You know what is best for me. Help me to be patient in the process of healing, and to trust that You are at work, even when I cannot see it. Lord, I also pray for the strength to forgive those who have caused me pain. I know that holding on to bitterness and resentment only deepens my suffering, and that You have called me to forgive as You have forgiven me. But I confess that forgiveness is difficult, especially when the wounds are deep. I pray that You will give me the grace to forgive those who have hurt me, and to release them into Your hands. Help me to let go of the anger and hurt, and to trust that You are the Righteous Judge who will bring justice in Your time. Give me the freedom that comes from forgiveness, and the peace that comes from letting go.

Father, I pray that You would help me to find meaning and purpose in my pain. It is so easy to become consumed by the pain and to lose sight of the bigger picture. But I know that You are a God who redeems all things, and that You can bring good out of even the most difficult circumstances. I pray that You will help me to see how You are at work in my pain, and to discover the ways in which You are using my suffering to shape me, to grow me, and to draw me closer to You. Give me the grace to embrace the lessons that You are teaching me, and the faith to trust that You are using my pain for a greater purpose. Lord, I pray for the grace to continue to hope in You. It is easy to lose hope when the pain is great and the road ahead seems long and uncertain. But I know that You are the God of hope, who fills us with all joy and peace in believing, so that we may abound in hope by the power of the Holy Spirit. I pray that You will renew my hope, and that You will help me to hold fast to the promises of Your Word. Remind me that You are faithful, that You are good, and that You have a future and hope for me. Help me to trust in Your timing, and to believe that You are working all things together for my good.

Father, I thank You for hearing my prayer, and for being with me during my pain. I know that You are a God who is near to the brokenhearted, and who saves those who are crushed in spirit. I thank You for Your love, your mercy, and Your grace, which sustain me in my darkest moments. I pray that You will continue to be my strength, my comfort, and my guide, and that You will lead me through this season of pain into a place of healing, wholeness, and peace. In Jesus' name, I pray. Amen.

Chapter Five
Betrayal

Betrayal is something that is often hard to recover from, especially when it is caused by those you hold close to you. I never thought in a million years the person that I grew to love as a family member would betrayal me by the harsh act he committed. I was stripped of something that I could never get back. I was stripped of my identity and due to this my faith in God was shaken to the core. Betrayal by loved ones whether by family members or close friends is among the most devastating experiences a person can endure. This form of betrayal cuts deep because it comes from those who are supposed to love, protect, and support us. When trust is shattered by those we hold dear, it leaves emotional scars that can take years, or even a lifetime, to heal. This chapter explores the profound impact of betrayal by loved ones, examining its emotional and psychological consequences, the ways it challenges our perception of relationships, and the journey toward healing and forgiveness.

The emotional toll of betrayal by family and friends is immense. These are the people we trust implicitly, those we turn to in times of need and rely on for support and comfort. When they betray that trust, the emotional impact is multifaceted, encompassing feelings of anger, sadness, confusion, and a deep sense of loss. Anger is often the initial response to betrayal. It is a natural reaction to the hurt and injustice inflicted by someone we trusted. This anger can be overwhelming, fueling a desire for retribution or justice. However, it can also become consuming if not addressed, leading to prolonged bitterness and resentment. The betrayal of a loved one can evoke a unique kind of anger because it feels personal, targeting the very heart of our emotional lives.

Sadness follows closely behind, as the reality of the betrayal sinks in. This sadness is not just about the specific act of betrayal but also about the loss of the relationship as it once was. The bond that was built on trust and mutual respect is now tainted, and the sense of security and love that once existed is shattered. This sadness can lead to grief, as we mourn the loss of what we thought the relationship was and come to terms with its new, damaged state. Confusion often accompanies betrayal, particularly when it comes from someone, we believe would never hurt us. We may find ourselves questioning our judgment, wondering how we could have been so wrong about someone we loved and trusted. This confusion can extend to our understanding of the relationship itself, leading us to reexamine past interactions and question whether there were signs we missed. This process of questioning can be emotionally exhausting, as it forces us to confront uncomfortable truths about ourselves and those we care about.

The emotional pain of betrayal can also lead to a profound sense of loss. This loss is not just about the relationship but also about the sense of identity and stability that the relationship provided. When a loved one betrays us, it can feel as though the ground has been pulled out from under us, leaving us adrift in a sea of uncertainty. The loss of trust can be particularly damaging, as it erodes the foundation of our relationships and can make it difficult to trust others in the future. Betrayal by family and friends also challenges our perception of relationships and the people within them. We are often socialized to believe that family is a safe haven, a source of unconditional love and support. Similarly, close friendships are built on the premise of mutual trust, loyalty, and care. When these core relationships are breached by betrayal, it forces us to reconsider these fundamental beliefs.

Family Betrayal: Betrayal within the family is especially painful because family relationships are typically seen as the most enduring and unbreakable. Families are supposed to be our first source of love, protection, and identity. When a family member betrays us whether through lies, deceit, or abandonment it can feel like a violation of the very essence of what family is supposed to be. This kind of betrayal can lead to a crisis of identity, as we grapple with the idea that those who are supposed to love us unconditionally have chosen to hurt us instead. It can also create a sense of alienation, as we may feel disconnected from the very people who are supposed to be our closest allies.

Friendship Betrayal: Betrayal by a close friend can be equally devastating. Friendships are often formed by choice, based on shared values, interests, and mutual respect. When a friend betrays us, it can feel like a rejection of who we are as individuals. The trust that was built over time is shattered, leaving us to question not only the integrity of the friend but also our ability to judge character. This kind of betrayal can make us wary of forming new friendships or trusting others, as the fear of being hurt again looms large. Both family and friendship betrayals can lead to a general mistrust of others. Once we have experienced betrayal from those we love, it becomes difficult to trust others, even those who have not wronged us. We may become guarded, putting up emotional walls to protect ourselves from future harm. This self-protective behavior, while understandable, can also lead to isolation and loneliness, as we push others away out of fear of being hurt again. Healing from betrayal is a complex and deeply personal journey. It involves not only coming to terms with the pain and loss but also finding a way to move forward, whether that involves rebuilding the relationship or letting it go. Central to this process is the concept of forgiveness, which is often misunderstood and difficult to achieve.

Acceptance: The first step in healing is accepting the reality of betrayal. This involves acknowledging the pain and hurt caused by the betrayal and allowing oneself to fully experience those emotions. Denying or minimizing the betrayal only prolongs the healing process, as it prevents us from dealing with the pain head-on. Acceptance also means letting go of the need to understand why the betrayal happened, as not all betrayals have clear explanations or reasons.

Self-reflection is a crucial part of the healing process. It involves examining our own role in the relationship and understanding how we may have contributed to the dynamics that led to the betrayal. This is not about blaming ourselves for the betrayal but rather about gaining insight into how we can learn and grow from the experience. Self-reflection also allows us to identify patterns in our relationships, helping us to avoid similar situations in the future.

Setting Boundaries: Rebuilding trust, if possible, requires setting clear boundaries. This involves communicating our needs and expectations to the person who betrayed us and ensuring that those boundaries are respected. Setting boundaries is an act of self-care and self-respect, as it allows us to protect ourselves from further harm. If the person who betrayed us is unwilling or unable to respect those boundaries, it may be necessary to distance ourselves from the relationship.

Forgiveness: Forgiveness is often seen as the goal of the healing process, but it is important to understand that forgiveness does not mean forgetting or excusing the betrayal. Rather, forgiveness is about letting go of the anger and resentment that keeps us bound to the pain of the betrayal. It is a process that takes time and may involve small steps, such as forgiving the person for specific actions or behaviors. Forgiveness is also a gift we give ourselves, as it allows us to move forward without being weighed down by the burden of the past.

Moving Forward: Whether or not forgiveness is achieved, the final step in healing is moving forward. This may involve rebuilding the relationship with the person who betrayed us, or it may mean letting go and moving on. Moving forward also means opening ourselves up to new relationships, despite the fear of being hurt again. It is about finding the courage to trust once more and to believe in the goodness of others.

Betrayal by family members and friends we love is one of the most painful experiences we can endure. It challenges our trust in others, our perception of relationships, and our sense of identity. The emotional and psychological impact of such betrayal is profound, leading to feelings of anger, sadness, confusion, and loss. However, through acceptance, self-reflection, boundary-setting, and forgiveness, it is possible to heal from the pain of betrayal and to move forward with renewed strength and resilience. While the scars of betrayal may never fully disappear, they can become a testament to our ability to endure, grow, and find hope in the face of adversity

A Prayer for Love in Spite of Betrayal

Heavenly Father,

I come before You today with a heart that is heavy, burdened by the pain of betrayal. Someone I trusted, someone I loved, has wounded me deeply, and I struggle to understand how I can move forward. Yet, in this moment of pain and confusion, I turn to You, the source of all love and strength, asking for Your guidance, Your comfort, and Your grace. Help me, Lord, to love even in the midst of betrayal, to reflect Your boundless love in my life, and to find peace in the process.
Lord, you have commanded us to love one another as You have loved us. This commandment is simple in words but profoundly difficult in practice, especially when we have been hurt by those we love. I confess that my heart is struggling to forgive and to love. The betrayal I have experienced has left me feeling angry, hurt, and disillusioned. Yet, I know that You are calling me to something greater. You are calling me to love, even when it is hard, even when it seems impossible.
Father, I ask for Your strength to love in spite of betrayal. My own strength is not enough; I am weak, and the pain sometimes overwhelms me. But I know that Your power is made perfect in weakness. I pray that You will fill me with Your strength, that I may love as You have loved me unconditionally, selflessly, and sacrificially. Help me to see beyond my pain and to remember that love is not just a feeling but a choice, a commitment to act with kindness and compassion, even when it is difficult.
Lord, I pray for the grace to forgive. Forgiveness is the cornerstone of love, and yet it is one of the hardest things to do when we have been betrayed. I know that You have called me to forgive as You have forgiven me, but I confess that I am struggling to let go of the hurt and the anger. I ask for Your help, Lord, to release the bitterness and resentment that have taken root in my heart. Teach me to forgive, not because the other person deserves it, but because You have forgiven me of far greater sins. Help me to understand that forgiveness is not about excusing the wrong but about freeing myself from the chains of anger and hurt that keep me bound. Father, give me a heart of compassion. In the wake of betrayal, it is easy to become hardened and defensive, to protect myself from further hurt by closing off my heart. But I know that this is not what You desire for me. You have called me

to have a heart that is soft and compassionate, even toward those who have hurt me. I pray that You would open my heart to see the person who betrayed me as You see them—not just as someone who has wronged me, but as someone who is also in need of Your love and grace. Help me to remember that we are all broken and in need of Your healing. Give me the compassion to see beyond the hurt and to extend love and grace, even when it is not deserved.

Lord, I pray for wisdom and discernment as I navigate this relationship. Loving despite betrayal does not mean ignoring the hurt or pretending that everything is okay. It does not mean allowing myself to be repeatedly hurt or mistreated. I ask for Your wisdom, Lord, to know how to love in a way that is healthy and honoring to You. Help me to set appropriate boundaries that protect my heart while still allowing me to show love and grace. Guide me in my interactions with the person who betrayed me, so that I may respond with both truth and love. Give me the discernment to know when to speak and when to remain silent, when to reach out and when to step back.

Father, I also pray for healing for myself and for the one who betrayed me. Betrayal leaves deep wounds, not just for the one who was betrayed but often for the betrayer as well. I ask for Your healing touch on my heart, Lord, that You would mend the broken places and restore what has been lost. Heal me from the pain of the betrayal and help me to trust again not just in others but in Your goodness and Your plan for my life. I also pray for the one who betrayed me, that You would bring healing to their heart as well. Whatever led them to this act of betrayal, I pray that You would meet them in their brokenness and bring about transformation and renewal in their life.

Lord, help me to trust in Your justice. Betrayal often leaves us feeling wronged, and the desire for justice can be overwhelming. But I know that true justice belongs to You. You are the righteous Judge who sees all and knows all. Help me to release my need for revenge or retribution and to trust that You will bring about justice in Your time and in Your way. Remind me that my role is not to seek vengeance but to love, to forgive, and to trust in Your perfect plan.

Father, I pray for the grace to love myself during this pain. Betrayal can often lead to feelings of inadequacy and self-doubt. I may find myself questioning my worth or wondering if I did something to deserve this hurt. But I know that my worth is not determined by the actions of others but by the love You have for me. Help me to see myself as You see me fearfully and wonderfully made, deeply loved, and worthy of respect and kindness. Give me the grace to care for myself, to set healthy boundaries, and to seek out the support I need as I navigate this difficult time.

Lord, I ask for Your peace. The turmoil of betrayal can leave my heart and mind in a state of constant unrest. I may find myself replaying the betrayal over and over in my mind, unable to find peace. But I know that You are the Prince of Peace, and You have promised to give peace to those who seek You. I pray that You would calm my heart and mind, that You would silence the voices of fear and doubt, and that You would fill me with Your perfect peace, a peace that surpasses all understanding. Help me to rest in the knowledge that You are in control, and that You are working all things together for my good.

Father, I thank You for Your love, which is steadfast and unchanging. In a world where betrayal and hurt are all too common, your love is a constant source of hope and strength. I thank You that Your love never fails, and that nothing can separate me from Your love not even the deepest betrayal. Help me to keep my eyes fixed on You, to draw strength from Your love, and to reflect that love in all my relationships. I thank You for the work You are doing in my heart, even during this pain, and I trust that You are bringing about good in ways that I cannot yet see.

Lord, I surrender this situation to You. I surrender to my pain, my anger, my confusion, and my desire for justice. I lay it all at Your feet, trusting that You will take this brokenness and turn it into something beautiful. I ask that You continue to work in my heart, to soften the hard places, and to fill me with Your love. Help me to love in spite of betrayal, to forgive as You have forgiven me, and to walk in the freedom and peace that comes from trusting in You.

In Jesus' name, I pray. Amen.

Chapter Six
Forgiveness

Forgiveness is a profound and transformative process, especially during moments of intense hurt, pain, and despair. It is not merely an act of letting go but a complex emotional and psychological journey that can lead to personal growth and healing. Understanding the importance of forgiveness, the challenges it presents, and practical steps to cultivate it can provide valuable insights into navigating difficult times. Forgiving during times of hurt, pain, and despair is undoubtedly challenging. The initial reaction to betrayal or harm is often one of anger, sadness, or disbelief, making it difficult to even consider forgiveness. The emotional intensity of these experiences can overshadow the ability to rationally approach the situation.

One of the significant challenges is the perception of injustice. When someone has been deeply wronged, it can seem as though forgiveness is an endorsement of harmful behavior. This perception can be particularly strong if the harm was severe or if the perpetrator shows no remorse. The internal struggle to reconcile the desire for justice with the act of forgiveness can be overwhelming. Another challenge is the fear of vulnerability. Forgiveness often requires individuals to confront their pain and the possibility of being hurt again. The fear of reopening old wounds or of being perceived as weak can hinder the willingness to forgive.

Forgiveness is not an easy path, but it is a necessary one for healing and growth. When we are hurt by others, our natural instinct may be to harbor resentment and bitterness. However, by choosing to forgive, we free ourselves from the weight of these negative emotions. Forgiveness is not about condoning the actions of those who have wronged us, but about releasing ourselves from the prison of their transgressions. It is a courageous and empowering act, one that allows us to move forward with a renewed sense of peace and clarity. Through the process of forgiveness, we can find the strength to let go of the past and embrace a future filled with hope and possibility

Forgiveness is a powerful act that can lead to profound personal growth and inner healing. While it may be tempting to hold onto resentment towards those who have hurt us, doing so ultimately serves only to drain us emotionally and prevent true reconciliation. Importantly, forgiveness does not mean condoning the hurtful actions of others or excusing their wrongdoing. Rather, it is the process of letting go of the anger and bitterness, allowing us to move forward with empathy, compassion, and a renewed sense of freedom. By embracing forgiveness, we empower ourselves to break the cycle of hurt and find the courage to build healthier, more fulfilling relationships.

When someone has wronged us, it can be difficult to let go of the hurt and resentment we feel. However, learning to forgive is an essential step in moving forward and finding peace. The first step is to take the time to reflect on the situation and try to understand the other person's perspective. What was their motivation? What might have been going on in their life that led them to act in that way? By cultivating empathy, we can begin to see the situation through a different lens. At the same time, it's important to acknowledge our own feelings of pain or betrayal, but to avoid dwelling on them. Forgiveness is not about denying our emotions, but about consciously choosing to let go of the hurt and move forward. With time and effort, we can learn to release negative energy and find the strength to forgive.

Additionally, the process of forgiveness is not always linear. Emotions can be unpredictable, and the journey towards forgiveness can involve setbacks and relapses into anger or sadness. This non-linear nature of forgiveness can make the process feel even more daunting. Forgiveness is a central theme in the Bible, deeply embedded in its teachings and narratives. From the Old Testament to the New Testament, the concept of forgiveness is portrayed as essential for spiritual and communal harmony. Understanding forgiveness from a biblical perspective involves exploring its scriptural foundations, the example set by Jesus Christ, and the implications for believers.

Forgiveness is a transformative act that can profoundly improve our mental and physical well-being. When we let go of resentment and bitterness towards those who have wronged us, we free ourselves from the heavy burden of negative emotions. This inner peace and freedom can have a remarkable impact on our overall health, reducing stress, anxiety, and even physical ailments. Furthermore, the ability to forgive strengthens our relationships and helps us navigate conflicts more effectively, leading to deeper, more meaningful connections with others. Ultimately, the decision to forgive is a powerful choice that grants us a greater sense of inner calm and personal growth, allowing us to live more fulfilling lives.

A Prayer for Forgiveness & Letting Go

Dear Heavenly Father,

We come before You today with heavy hearts, seeking Your divine guidance and grace. We have been burdened by wounds—some inflicted by others, and some that we have carried ourselves. We recognize that these wounds, whether deep or superficial, hinder our growth and our ability to live fully in Your love. As we stand before You in prayer, we ask for the strength to forgive and the wisdom to let go of the hurt that binds us.

Lord, you know the pain we carry. You understand the weight of our grievances and the bitterness that sometimes seeps into our souls. We confess that holding onto hurt has been a comfort in its own way, as if it were a shield protecting us from further pain. But, Father, we know that this shield is heavy and cumbersome. It keeps us from the freedom and joy that You desire for us. Help us, O Lord, to set down this burden and embrace the peace that only You can provide.

Teach us, dear Father, the true meaning of forgiveness. We know that forgiveness is not merely a gesture of releasing someone from a debt they owe us. It is a profound act of love and mercy, reflecting the boundless grace You have shown us. Help us to understand that forgiving does not mean forgetting or condoning the wrongs done to us but choosing to release the grip of anger and resentment from our hearts. It is about reclaiming our peace and allowing Your healing presence to transform our pain into compassion.

We pray for the courage to face the source of our hurt, whether it be a person, a situation, or even ourselves. Give us the strength to confront these issues with honesty and humility. Let Your wisdom guides our words and actions, so that they may be infused with Your love and understanding. Let us not be overwhelmed by the magnitude of our pain but be empowered by Your Spirit to transcend it.

In moments when the pain resurfaces, remind us of the strength that comes from Your grace. Help us to practice forgiveness daily, knowing that it is a journey rather than a destination. We ask for Your guidance to make this a continual part of our lives, rather than a one-time act. Let forgiveness become our second nature, as natural as breathing, so that it may flow from us to others as freely as it does from You to us.

Lord, we also pray for those who have hurt us. We ask that You soften their hearts and lead them towards Your truth and healing. Help us to see them through Your eyes, recognizing their own struggles and imperfections. Just as we seek Your forgiveness, we hope that they, too, may find solace and transformation through Your grace. Let our act of forgiving them be a testament to Your love and a catalyst for reconciliation. Help us to let go of our desire for revenge or retribution. Remind us that vengeance belongs to You alone, and our role is to live in harmony with Your will. Teach us to replace our anger with understanding and our resentment with kindness. In doing so, we align ourselves with Your divine purpose and become vessels of Your peace in a world that so desperately needs it.

Heavenly Father, as we embark on this journey of forgiveness, let Your love be the compass that guides us. Fill our hearts with Your peace and renew our spirits with Your joy. Transform our pain into a powerful testimony of Your healing and grace. Let our lives reflect Your mercy, shining brightly during darkness and hurt.

We pray this in the name of Your Son, Jesus Christ, who taught us to love our enemies and pray for those who persecute us. May His example inspire us to live lives of true forgiveness and unwavering love.

Amen.

Chapter Seven
Love Thy Enemy (Æmbracing Love Amidst Wrongdoing)

Loving one's enemies is a profound and challenging directive found in various philosophical and religious traditions, particularly in Christianity. The call to love those who have wronged us or who oppose us runs counter to natural inclinations of retaliation and resentment. This statement explores the importance of loving one's enemies, examining the transformative power of such love and its implications for personal growth and societal harmony.

The concept of loving one's enemies is most prominently articulated in the teachings of Jesus Christ. In the Sermon on the Mount, Jesus delivers a radical message in Matthew 5:43-44: "You have heard that it was said, 'Love your neighbor and hate your enemy.' But I tell you, love your enemies and pray for those who persecute you." This directive challenges conventional wisdom and calls for a higher standard of love—one that extends beyond mere tolerance to genuine compassion. To love one's enemies means to hold no ill will towards them, despite the wrongs they have committed. It requires a deliberate choice to act with kindness, to seek their well-being, and to maintain a posture of forgiveness.

This type of love is not based on the merit or behavior of the enemy but on a commitment to live out the values of compassion and grace. Loving your enemies has profound implications for personal growth. It involves a process of overcoming negative emotions such as anger, bitterness, and hatred. By choosing to love rather than retaliate, individuals can experience a release from the emotional burdens that come with harboring resentment. This act of forgiveness fosters inner peace and helps in breaking the cycle of negativity that can otherwise consume one's life.

Practically, this means transforming the internal narrative from one of victimhood to one of empowerment. When one chooses to love, they reclaim control over their emotional state, shifting from being a passive recipient of harm to an active agent of positive change. The act of loving one's enemies can lead to reconciliation and healing in strained relationships. By extending kindness and compassion, individuals create an environment conducive to dialogue and mutual understanding. This approach can open doors to repair and renewal, allowing for the possibility of resolving conflicts and rebuilding trust.

Moreover, such actions can have a ripple effect, influencing others to adopt a similar stance of forgiveness and compassion. This can gradually transform hostile environments into more harmonious ones, promoting a culture of empathy and respect. Loving one's enemies can be incredibly challenging due to natural instincts of self-preservation and justice. The instinct to defend oneself or seek revenge can be strong, and it may require substantial effort to counter these impulses. The key is to recognize these instincts without being controlled by them.

Practical strategies for overcoming these instincts include mindfulness practices, prayer, and seeking support from faith communities or counselors. These resources can provide guidance and strength in maintaining a loving posture even in the face of adversity. Loving one's enemies does not mean tolerating ongoing harm or abuse. It is important to set healthy boundaries to protect oneself from further hurt. This might involve limiting contact with those who have caused significant harm while still maintaining a posture of forgiveness and compassion.

Setting boundaries allows individuals to address harmful behaviors without succumbing to bitterness. It is a way to balance love with self-respect and personal safety, ensuring that the act of forgiveness does not lead to further victimization. The practice of loving one's enemies can inspire others to adopt similar values, creating a ripple effect of positive change. Stories of forgiveness and compassion can serve as powerful testimonies, motivating individuals to rise above hatred and contribute to a more inclusive and understanding world.

This inspirational aspect of loving one's enemies highlights the potential for individual actions to influence collective attitudes and behaviors. It underscores the idea that personal acts of love and forgiveness can drive significant societal transformation. Loving one's enemies, despite the wrongs they have committed, is a challenging yet profoundly transformative practice. It requires overcoming natural instincts, setting healthy boundaries, and distinguishing forgiveness from the neglect of justice. However, the rewards of such love are manifold personal peace, relational healing, and societal harmony. By embracing the call to love our enemies, we align ourselves with higher principles of compassion and grace. This practice not only reflects divine love but also has the potential to inspire broader positive change, fostering a more empathetic and just world. In loving our enemies, we embody the essence of true forgiveness, demonstrating the power of love to transcend adversity and create a more harmonious existence.

A Prayer for Embracing Love

Heavenly Father,

We approach Your throne of grace with hearts full of reverence and humility, seeking Your divine wisdom and strength. Your command to "love thy enemy" challenges us profoundly, and we come before You in earnest prayer, asking for the courage and grace to embrace this divine mandate. It is easy to love those who love us, but You call us to a higher standard—to love even those who have wronged us and caused us pain.

Lord, we acknowledge that loving our enemies is one of the most difficult tasks You have set before us. The pain inflicted by others can create deep wounds in our hearts, and often, the desire for justice or retaliation overshadows our ability to respond with love. We confess that, in our human weakness, we struggle with resentment, anger, and the desire to hold onto our grievances. Yet, we know that Your call to love transcends our understanding and is an essential part of our journey of faith.

Help us, O Lord, to understand the profound meaning of loving our enemies. Teach us that love is not merely an emotion but a deliberate choice and action. It is about extending grace and kindness, even when it feels undeserved. It is about seeking the well-being of others; despite the wrongs they have committed against us. Let our love reflect Your boundless love for us, which is unconditional and unending.

Father, give us the strength to overcome the bitterness that may reside in our hearts. When we are hurt, it is natural to want to protect ourselves and to distance ourselves from those who have caused us pain. Yet, you call us to break down these barriers and to reach out with compassion. Help us to remember that every person is a creation of Your love and is deserving of Your grace, regardless of their actions. Guide us in finding ways to show love to those who have wronged us. Grant us the wisdom to know how to respond with kindness and the discernment to act in ways that reflect Your character. It might be through words of encouragement, acts of service, or simply offering prayers for their well-being. Let us be instruments of Your peace and agents of reconciliation, working towards healing and understanding even during conflict.

Lord, we also ask for humility to recognize our own faults and shortcomings. Just as we seek forgiveness from others, let us not forget to extend forgiveness and love to those who have hurt us. Help us to see them as fellow travelers on the journey of life, each in need of Your grace. Let this understanding soften our hearts and lead us to respond with empathy and compassion.

In moments when loving our enemies feels impossible, remind us of the example of Your Son, Jesus Christ. He loved those who betrayed Him, mocked Him, and nailed Him to the cross. His ultimate act of love was in His forgiveness of those who wronged Him, offering them a path to redemption. Let His sacrifice be our inspiration and guide us in extending the same grace to others.

We pray for those who have wronged us, asking that You work in their hearts and lead them towards Your truth. Help us to release any desire for vengeance or retribution, trusting that You are the ultimate judge and that Your justice is perfect. May our acts of love and forgiveness serve as a testimony to Your transformative power and bring about reconciliation and healing.

Father, let our love be more than a passive sentiment. Let it be a powerful force that changes lives and brings glory to Your name. Empower us to live out Your command to love our enemies with sincerity and joy. As we embrace this divine call, may we grow closer to You and reflect Your love in all that we do.

We offer this prayer in the name of Your Son, Jesus Christ, who taught us to love not only our friends but our enemies as well. May His example be our guide and His Spirit our strength.

Amen.

Chapter Eight
I Am a Survivor

Life can be profoundly challenging, especially for those who face the heart-wrenching experiences of divorce, domestic violence, rape, and childhood trauma. These adversities can leave deep emotional scars, impacting one's ability to trust, love, and live fully. Yet, amid such profound suffering, the journey to healing and accepting love back into one's life is possible. This chapter explores the paths to recovery from these traumas, emphasizing resilience, self-compassion, and the gradual reawakening of one's capacity for love. Each of these experiences—divorce, domestic violence, rape, and childhood trauma brings its own set of challenges and emotional burdens. Divorce, while often framed as a relational shift, can also feel like a profound personal failure, resulting in loss of identity and self-worth. Domestic violence introduces a pattern of control and fear that undermines a person's sense of safety and self-esteem. Rape, a traumatic violation, carries with it deep feelings of shame, powerlessness, and mistrust. Childhood trauma, whether through abuse, neglect, or other forms of neglect, often shapes one's worldview and self-concept in ways that persist into adulthood.

Each of these traumas affects the way individuals relate to themselves and others. They can foster a pervasive sense of insecurity and unworthiness, which might make the idea of opening up to love again to seem daunting or even impossible. Understanding these impacts is crucial for healing, as it allows survivors to approach their recovery with compassion and patience. The first step towards healing is acknowledging the pain. Trauma survivors often grapple with feelings of isolation and denial. Society's tendency to downplay or stigmatize these experiences can exacerbate these feelings. Validating one's pain is essential for recovery. Therapy can provide a safe space for survivors to process their emotions and experiences. Licensed professionals can offer techniques for managing trauma responses and help individuals understand their feelings without judgment.

Healing from trauma is rarely a solitary journey. Building a supportive network of friends, family, or support groups can be instrumental. Such networks offer emotional support, validation, and practical assistance.

Trusted friends or family members can provide a listening ear and a shoulder to lean on, while support groups offer the opportunity to connect with others who have faced similar challenges. These connections can combat feelings of isolation and provide practical advice on navigating the recovery process.

Self-compassion involves treating oneself with the same kindness and understanding that one would offer a loved one. It requires recognizing that experiencing trauma does not diminish one's worth. Self-care practices, such as mindfulness, physical exercise, and engaging in hobbies, can help mitigate the stress and emotional pain associated with trauma. Creating routines that promote physical and emotional well-being can also aid in rebuilding a sense of normalcy and control Trauma can severely impact one's self-esteem and ability to trust others. Rebuilding trust, both in oneself and in others, is a gradual process. It involves setting small, achievable goals and recognizing personal growth along the way. Cognitive-behavioral strategies can assist in challenging and reframing negative beliefs about oneself. Rebuilding self-esteem also involves celebrating small victories and acknowledging the strength it takes to face and overcome daily challenges. Reengaging with love and relationships requires a cautious approach. Survivors should allow themselves to take gradual steps towards forming new connections. This might start with building platonic relationships and slowly expanding to romantic possibilities. It's essential to prioritize personal readiness and comfort, ensuring that new relationships are built on trust and mutual respect.

Setting and maintaining healthy boundaries is crucial for any relationship, particularly for those who have experienced trauma. Boundaries help protect one's emotional well-being and provide a sense of control and safety. Open communication about needs and limits in relationships can foster a healthy dynamic where both partners feel respected and valued. Embracing love again involves a willingness to be vulnerable. Vulnerability is not a weakness but a strength that allows for genuine connection and intimacy. It involves opening about one's fears, hopes, and past experiences in a way that fosters understanding and closeness. Embracing vulnerability is a step towards trusting others and allowing oneself to experience the fullness of love and connection. Professional therapy can be a valuable resource in navigating the complexities of re-entering the world of love and relationships.

Therapists can provide tools for managing anxiety and fear, as well as strategies for building healthy relationships. They can also assist in addressing any lingering trauma that might impact one's ability to fully engage in love and intimacy. The journey from surviving trauma to embracing love is deeply personal and multifaceted. It requires acknowledging and validating the pain, seeking support, practicing self-care, and gradually rebuilding trust and self-esteem. Embracing love amidst past wounds is not about forgetting or minimizing the pain but about finding the strength to move forward and open one's heart again. Healing is a process, and it's important to be patient with oneself. Every step taken towards recovery is a testament to resilience and courage. By addressing the impacts of trauma, rebuilding one's sense of self, and allowing love to reenter one's life, survivors can experience profound healing and joy. The capacity to love and be loved, even after deep pain, is a powerful testament to the strength of the human spirit and the transformative power of grace and self-compassion.

A Prayer for Survival & Hope

Heavenly Father,

We come before You in humble reverence, seeking Your divine presence and unwavering support as we navigate the trials and tribulations of our lives. Each of us faces moments of great struggle, hardship, and uncertainty, and in these times, we find ourselves yearning for Your guidance and strength. We ask for Your comforting embrace and the resilience to endure, knowing that with You by our side, we can face any challenge that comes our way.

Lord, you are our refuge and strength, a very present help in times of trouble. We recognize that in our moments of weakness, when the weight of our burdens seems too great to bear, you are our source of hope and renewal. We seek Your presence to fortify our spirits and grant us the courage to face our difficulties with faith and perseverance. Help us to remember that, even in the darkest of times, your light shines brightly, guiding us towards the path of healing and restoration. Grant us the strength to endure the trials that test our faith and resolve. When we feel overwhelmed by the challenges before us, remind us that You are our steadfast support. Infuse us with Your peace, which surpasses all understanding, so that we may find calm amidst the chaos and solace in our struggles. Let us draw strength from Your promises, knowing that You Walk with us through every storm, providing us with the courage to persevere and the wisdom to overcome.

In moments of despair, when hope seems distant and the path ahead is obscured, let Your presence be a beacon of light. May Your grace sustain us when we feel depleted, and Your love surround us when we feel isolated. Teach us to lean on Your strength and trust in Your plan, even when the journey is difficult and the outcome uncertain. Help us to surrender our worries and fears to You, trusting that your divine wisdom and love will guide us towards the resolution and peace we seek.

Father, we also pray for the wisdom to seek support and the humility to accept help from others. Surround us with compassionate individuals who can offer encouragement, practical assistance, and a listening ear. Let us be open to the support of our community, understanding that Your provision often comes through the kindness of those around us. Grant us the discernment to recognize and embrace the resources and relationships that can aid us in our journey of survival.

As we face the trials of life, help us to remain focused on the lessons that each challenge brings. Teach us to see our struggles not as obstacles, but as opportunities for growth and transformation. Let us cultivate a spirit of gratitude, finding purpose and meaning even during adversity. May our experiences deepen our faith, strengthen our character, and draw us closer to You.

Lord, we lift up to you those who are currently struggling and in need of Your intervention. Whether they are facing financial hardship, health issues, emotional distress, or relational conflicts, we ask for Your healing touch and transformative power in their lives. May Your presence bring comfort to those who are suffering and hope to those who are weary. Let them experience Your peace and reassurance and grant them the strength to endure and overcome their challenges.

We also ask for Your guidance as we strive to be sources of support and encouragement to others. Help us to be instruments of Your love and compassion, reaching out to those in need and offering a helping hand. Empower us to reflect Your grace, providing comfort and strength to those who are struggling, and embodying the hope that comes from knowing You are with us in every circumstance.

As we move forward, may we continually seek Your presence and guidance. Let us place our trust in You, knowing that Your plans for us are filled with hope and a future. Strengthen our faith, renew our spirits, and grant us the resilience to face each day with courage and optimism. May Your love be our anchor, Your wisdom our guide, and Your peace our constant companion.

We offer this prayer in the name of Your Son, Jesus Christ, who demonstrated unwavering faith and strength in the face of His own trials. May His example inspire us to persevere with grace and courage, and may His love fill our hearts as we journey through life's challenges.

Amen.

Chapter Nine
I Am Worthy

In a world that often measures success by external achievements and social approval, understanding and embracing your intrinsic value can be a challenging yet profoundly rewarding journey. Self-worth refers to the inherent value you place on yourself, independent of external factors such as accomplishments, wealth, or others' opinions. Self-love, on the other hand, is the practice of caring for and nurturing yourself with the same compassion and understanding you would offer to a loved one. These concepts are fundamental to personal growth and well-being, as they provide the foundation for a fulfilling and balanced life. This chapter explores the importance of knowing your worth and loving your true self, examining the challenges that arise in this pursuit and offering strategies to cultivate a healthy sense of self.
Self-worth is the internal sense of being good enough and worthy of love and belonging from others. It's the belief that you are valuable regardless of what you achieve or how others perceive you. This concept is deeply influenced by various factors, including upbringing, societal expectations, and personal experiences. For example, individuals raised in nurturing environments where they were consistently affirmed and supported may develop a strong sense of self-worth. Conversely, those who grew up in environments where love was conditional or where they faced constant criticism may struggle with feelings of inadequacy.

The level of self-worth you hold can significantly influence your daily life and decision-making. A healthy sense of self-worth leads to confident and assertive behavior, as individuals who know their value are less likely to settle for less than they deserve in relationships, work, and other areas of life. They make choices that align with their values and are more resilient in the face of challenges. On the other hand, low self-worth can result in self-sabotaging behaviors, difficulty setting boundaries, and a tendency to seek validation from others, often leading to dissatisfaction and unhappiness. Despite the importance of self-worth, many people struggle to maintain a positive self-image due to various external and internal challenges. Societal pressures play a significant role in shaping perceptions of self-worth. In a culture that glorifies success, beauty, and material wealth, it's easy to fall into the trap of comparing oneself to others and feeling inadequate. Social media exacerbates this issue by presenting curated versions of other people's lives, leading to unrealistic standards and heightened insecurity. Internal challenges also pose significant obstacles to self-worth. Negative self-talk, self-doubt, and perfectionism are common issues that can erode one's sense of value. For instance, individuals who constantly criticize themselves for not meeting certain standards may struggle to recognize their worth. Perfectionism can be damaging as it sets unattainable goals, leading to feelings of failure and inadequacy when these goals are not met. These challenges can have a profound impact on mental and emotional health, contributing to anxiety, depression, and a general sense of dissatisfaction with life. Overcoming these obstacles requires a conscious effort to shift one's mindset and adopt healthier perspectives. Loving your true self involves accepting and appreciating yourself for who you are, including your strengths and imperfections. It's about recognizing that you are deserving of love, care, and respect, just as you are. Self-love is often misunderstood as selfishness, but it's the opposite. When you love yourself, you are better equipped to love others, as you are coming from a place of wholeness rather than neediness.

Self-love plays a crucial role in building resilience and confidence. When you have a strong foundation of self-love, you are less likely to be swayed by others' opinions or to seek validation from external sources. This internal strength allows you to navigate life's challenges with greater ease and to maintain your sense of self-worth even in difficult situations. Practicing self-love can take many forms, from engaging in self-care routines to setting boundaries that protect your well-being. Affirmations, for example, are a powerful tool for reinforcing positive beliefs about yourself. By regularly reminding yourself of your worth and capabilities, you can gradually shift your mindset and develop a more loving relationship with yourself. Cultivating self-worth and self-love requires intentional effort and practice. One effective strategy is to identify and challenge negative beliefs that undermine your sense of value. This might involve reflecting on the origins of these beliefs, questioning their validity, and replacing them with more positive, empowering thoughts. Cognitive-behavioral techniques, such as reframing negative thoughts, can be particularly helpful in this process.

Setting healthy boundaries in relationships is another important aspect of self-worth. When you value yourself, you recognize that you have the right to protect your time, energy, and emotional well-being. This means being selective about the people you allow into your life and being assertive in communicating your needs. Embracing imperfections is also key to loving your true self. No one is perfect, and striving for perfection can lead to unnecessary stress and dissatisfaction. Instead, practice self-compassion by treating yourself with the same kindness and understanding that you would offer to a friend. Acknowledge your flaws and mistakes, but don't let them define you. Remember that growth and learning often come from these experiences.

Also, surround yourself with supportive people who uplift and encourage you. Having a strong support system can reinforce your sense of worth and provide a buffer against negative influences. Seek out relationships that are based on mutual respect and understanding and let go of those that are toxic or draining. The benefits of knowing your worth and loving your true self are profound and far-reaching. Enhanced mental and emotional well-being is one of the most significant outcomes. When you have a healthy sense of self-worth, you are less likely to experience anxiety, depression, and other mental health issues. You are also more likely to have positive self-esteem and a more optimistic outlook on life.

Improved relationships are another benefit of embracing self-worth and self-love. When you value yourself, you are more likely to form healthy, balanced relationships where your needs are respected. You are less likely to tolerate mistreatment or settle for less than you deserve. This leads to more fulfilling and supportive connections with others. Finally, knowing your worth and loving your true self can lead to greater personal fulfillment and life satisfaction. When you are true to yourself and live in alignment with your values, you are more likely to pursue meaningful goals and achieve a sense of purpose. You are also more likely to experience joy and contentment, as you are not constantly striving to meet external expectations.

Finally, knowing your worth and loving your true self are essential components of a fulfilling and balanced life. By understanding your intrinsic value and cultivating self-love, you can overcome challenges, build resilience, and create a life that reflects your true potential. While the journey may not always be easy, the rewards of self-discovery and acceptance are immeasurable. As you continue this path, remember that you are deserving of love, care, and respect, just as you are. Embrace your worth, love yourself fully, and watch as your life transforms in beautiful and unexpected ways.

A Prayer for Self-Worth

Divine Creator,

I come before You today, humbly seeking Your guidance and love. I acknowledge that I am made in Your image, fearfully and wonderfully created. Yet, I sometimes struggle to see my worth, to feel the depth of my value as Your beloved child. Today, I ask for Your help in recognizing and embracing my true worth, not as the world sees me, but as You have always seen me. Help me to understand that my value is inherent, given by You, and not dependent on external achievements, appearances, or the approval of others. O Lord, you are the source of all love, the foundation upon which I stand. In Your infinite wisdom, you crafted every part of me, each strength, each weakness, each flaw, and each gift. You knew me before I was born, and You called me by name. I am not an accident or a mistake; I am a masterpiece of Your divine love.

Help me, O Lord, to internalize this truth. Let me feel the warmth of Your love in my heart, the certainty that I am enough because You made me. Let me see myself through Your eyes—eyes that are full of compassion, mercy, and unconditional love. When I am tempted to doubt my worth, remind me that I am precious in Your sight, not because of what I do, but simply because I am Yours.

Gracious Father, I carry wounds from the past, from times when I felt rejected, unloved, or insignificant. These experiences have left scars on my heart, and they have distorted the way I see myself. I have believed lies that I am not good enough, that I must earn my worth, or that I am somehow flawed beyond repair. These lies have taken root in my mind, and they have kept me from living fully in the freedom of Your love. Today, I ask for Your healing touch. Pour out Your grace upon me and cleanse me of these false beliefs. Uproot the lies and plant seeds of truth in their place. Help me to forgive those who have hurt me, and to forgive myself for the times I have failed to see my worth. Restore me, Lord, to the fullness of who You created me to be. Let Your healing light shine into every dark corner of my soul, so that I may walk in the light of Your truth. O God, in this journey toward self-worth, I know there will be challenges. There will be days when I feel weak, when the voices of doubt and insecurity grow loud. On those days, Lord, I pray for Your strength. Fortify me with Your Spirit, that I may stand firm in the truth of who I am in You.

Help me to resist the pressures of the world that seek to define me by superficial standards. When I am tempted to compare myself to others, remind me that I am unique, with a purpose that only I can fulfill. Give me the courage to embrace my individuality, to celebrate the gifts and talents You have bestowed upon me, and to pursue the path You have laid out for me.

May I draw strength from Your Word, which tells me that I am more than a conqueror through Christ who loves me. Let this truth be my anchor, my foundation, especially in times of trial and uncertainty. With You by my side, I know that I can overcome any obstacle, not because of my own strength, but because Your power is made perfect in my weakness. Heavenly Father, I know that my worth is not just about how I see myself, but also about how I live out the purpose You have given me. I pray for Your guidance as I seek to fulfill the calling You have placed on my life. Show me the way, Lord, and give me the wisdom to discern Your will.

Help me to use my gifts and talents for Your glory, to serve others with a heart full of love and compassion. Let my life reflect Your grace and goodness. As I walk in the path You have set before me, may I grow in confidence, knowing that I am doing the work You have prepared for me.

May I never forget that my worth is not measured by worldly success or recognition, but by my faithfulness to You and the love I share with others. Let my life be a testament to the truth that every person is valuable in Your eyes, and that true fulfillment comes from living in alignment with Your will.

I thank You for the work You are doing in my heart. I thank You for every step forward on this journey of self-discovery and self-worth. Even when the road is difficult, I am grateful that I do not walk it alone. Your presence is with me, guiding me, comforting me, and strengthening me every day.

Thank You for loving me so completely, for never giving up on me, even when I struggle to see my worth. Thank You for the gift of life, for the opportunities You give me to grow, to learn, and to become more of the person You created me to be. I am grateful for Your patience with me, for Your forgiveness, and for the grace that covers all my shortcomings.

Most of all, I thank You for the gift of Your Son, Jesus Christ, through whom I have been redeemed and made new. Because of Him, I know that I am loved with an everlasting love, a love that is unchanging and unbreakable. In Christ, I find my true identity, my true worth. I am a child of God, and that is enough.

Lord, as I close this prayer, I dedicate myself to living out the truth of my worth each day. Help me to walk in confidence, to love myself as You love me, and to extend that love to others. Let my life be a beacon of Your light, shining brightly in a world that so often forgets the value of every soul.

I surrender my insecurities, my doubts, and my fears to You. Fill me with Your peace, which surpasses all understanding. Guide my steps, and let Your love be the foundation of all that I do. I trust in Your perfect plan for my life, and I rest in the assurance that I am valuable, I am loved, I am worthy, because I am Yours.

In Your Holy Name, I pray.

Amen

Chapter Ten
No Turning Back

Life is a journey filled with both challenges and opportunities. As we travel along this path, we often find ourselves burdened by the weight of our past mistakes, regrets, and the pain of unfulfilled dreams. However, to fully embrace the future and the promises God has for us, it is essential to learn how to walk away from the past and move forward with hope and faith. I will help you explore the importance of letting go of the past, the spiritual and emotional benefits of embracing the future, and the ways in which we can trust in God's promises to guide us toward a life of purpose and fulfillment.

The past, with all its memories, experiences, and lessons, plays a significant role in shaping who we are. However, clinging to the past especially to negative experiences—can hinder our growth and prevent us from moving forward. Whether it's holding onto past mistakes, reliving painful experiences, or dwelling on missed opportunities, an attachment to the past can keep us stuck in a cycle of regret and self-doubt. One of the most powerful steps we can take in our spiritual journey is to release the past and allow God to heal our wounds. In Philippians 3:13-14, the Apostle Paul writes, "Brothers and sisters, I do not consider myself yet to have taken hold of it. But one thing I do: Forgetting what is behind and straining toward what is ahead, I press on toward the goal to win the prize for which God has called me heavenward in Christ Jesus." This scripture emphasizes the importance of forgetting what is behind and focusing on what lies ahead. By letting go of the past, we free ourselves to pursue the future that God has prepared for us.

Letting go of the past does not mean ignoring or denying the reality of what has happened. Instead, it involves acknowledging the past, learning from it, and choosing not to let it define or control us. It is a conscious decision to release the emotional and mental burdens that come with past experiences, allowing us to move forward with a renewed sense of purpose and direction. As we let go of the past, we open ourselves to the future and the endless possibilities it holds. The future is not just a continuation of the present; it is a canvas on which God can paint a new and beautiful picture for our lives. Embracing the future requires hope a confident expectation that God has good things in store for us.

Jeremiah 29:11 is a well-known verse that encapsulates this hope: "For I know the plans I have for you," declares the Lord, "plans to prosper you and not to harm you, plans to give you hope and a future." This promise from God assures us that the future is not something to be feared, but something to be eagerly anticipated. God's plans for us are filled with hope, prosperity, and well-being. By embracing the future with faith in God's promises, we can walk forward with confidence, knowing that our lives are in His hands. Hope is a powerful force that motivates us to keep moving forward, even when the path ahead is uncertain or challenging. It is through hope that we find the strength to persevere, to dream again, and to pursue the purpose that God has set before us. By placing our hope in God and His promises, we can navigate the unknown with the assurance that He is guiding our steps and that His plans for us are good.

As we move forward into the future, it is essential to trust in the promises God has made to us. The Bible is filled with promises that provide comfort, guidance, and assurance. These promises serve as a foundation for our faith, reminding us that God is faithful and that He will fulfill His word. One of the most profound promises is found in Romans 8:28: "And we know that in all things God works for the good of those who love Him, who have been called according to His purpose." This verse reassures us that, no matter what we face, God is working all things together for our good. Even when we encounter difficulties or setbacks, we can trust that God is orchestrating every detail of our lives to bring about His perfect plan.

Another powerful promise is found in Isaiah 43:18-19: "Forget the former things; do not dwell on the past. See, I am doing a new thing! Now it springs up; do you not perceive it? I am making a way in the wilderness and streams in the wasteland." This scripture encourages us to shift our focus from the past to the new things God is doing in our lives. It reminds us that God is always at work, creating new opportunities, opening new doors, and making a way where there seems to be no way. Trusting in God's promises requires faith, faith that God is who He says He is and that He will do what He has promised. This faith is not blind; it is rooted in our relationship with God and our understanding of His character. As we grow in our faith, we become more confident in God's ability to fulfill His promises, and we are more willing to step out in obedience, even when the future is uncertain.

Walking away from the past and moving forward into the future involves more than just hope and trust; it also requires action. Faith without works is dead (James 2:26), and so we must actively pursue the future God has for us by walking in obedience to His will. This means aligning our actions, decisions, and goals with God's purpose for our lives. Moving forward in faith and obedience involves taking practical steps to fulfill the calling God has placed on our lives. It may involve pursuing new opportunities, stepping out of our comfort zones, or making changes that align our lives more closely with God's will. It may also involve letting go of habits, relationships, or attitudes that no longer serve God's purpose in our lives.

As we take these steps, we can be assured that God is with us every step of the way. Deuteronomy 31:8 says, "The Lord Himself goes before you and will be with you; He will never leave you nor forsake you. Do not be afraid; do not be discouraged." This promise reminds us that we are never alone on our journey. God goes before us, preparing the way, and He walks beside us, providing strength and encouragement. walking away from the past and moving forward into the future is a vital part of our spiritual growth and journey with God. It requires us to let go of the burdens that weigh us down, embrace the future with hope, and trust in the promises God has made to us. By walking in faith and obedience, we align our lives with God's purpose and open ourselves to the abundant blessings He has in store for us. As we continue this journey, may we be reminded of the words of the Apostle Paul: "But one thing I do: Forgetting what is behind and straining toward what is ahead, I press on toward the goal to win the prize for which God has called me heavenward in Christ Jesus" (Philippians 3:13-14). Let us press on, confident that the future God has prepared for us is filled with hope, purpose, and the fulfillment of His promises.

A Prayer for No Turning Back: Moving Forward in Faith and Trust in God

Heavenly Father,

I come before You today with a heart full of gratitude and humility. I recognize that You are the author and finisher of my faith, the one who holds my future in Your hands. As I stand at this crossroads in my life, I ask for Your guidance and strength. I am determined, Lord, not to look back but to move forward in faith, trusting in Your perfect plan for my life. Help me, O God, to keep my eyes fixed on You, to walk boldly in the path You have set before me, and to never turn back to the things that hold me captive. May my life be a testament to Your faithfulness and a reflection of my unwavering trust in You. O Lord, you are the sovereign ruler of the universe, the one who spoke the world into existence and who holds all things together by the power of Your word. You know the beginning from the end, and nothing is hidden from Your sight. I acknowledge that You have a purpose and a plan for my life, a plan that is good, perfect, and pleasing.

Father, I thank You for the times You have guided me, even when I did not understand the way forward. You have been my light in the darkness, my anchor in the storm, and my refuge in times of trouble. I trust that You will continue to guide me as I move forward, knowing that Your ways are higher than my ways and Your thoughts higher than my thoughts. As I take each step into the future, I ask for Your wisdom to discern the path You have laid out for me. Help me to hear Your voice clearly, to follow Your lead without hesitation, and to trust in Your timing. When I am tempted to turn back to the familiar, remind me that You are calling me to something greater. Give me the courage to let go of the past and to embrace the new things You are doing in my life.

Gracious God, I confess that there are times when the past calls out to me, tempting me to return to old habits, old mindsets, and old ways of living. But I know, Lord, that You have called me to move forward, to press on toward the goal for which You have called me heavenward in Christ Jesus. I pray for the strength to let go of anything that holds me back whether it be past mistakes, regrets, or fears. I release these burdens into Your hands, trusting that You can redeem every part of my story for Your glory. Help me to see my past through the lens of

Your grace, understanding that it does not define me, but rather, it has prepared me for the future You have in store.

Father, as I embrace the future, fill me with a sense of anticipation and excitement for what lies ahead. I believe that You are doing a new thing in my life, and I want to be ready to receive it. Open my eyes to the opportunities that You place before me and give me the faith to step into them with confidence. When the road ahead seems uncertain, remind me that You are already there, preparing the way for me. I know that moving forward requires not just faith, but also obedience. I pray for a heart that is fully surrendered to Your will, a heart that desires to please You above all else. Help me to walk in the light of Your truth, to live according to Your word, and to follow the leading of Your Holy Spirit.

When I face challenges or obstacles, may I remember that You are with me, strengthening me and equipping me to overcome. Give me the perseverance to keep going, even when the journey is difficult. Let my faith be unwavering, rooted in the knowledge that You are faithful to Your promises.

I pray that my life would reflect my trust in You, that others would see in me a person who is unshaken by the storms of life because I am anchored in Your love. May my actions, my decisions, and my words all testify to the fact that I am moving forward with You, leaving behind the things that no longer serve Your purpose in my life. Lord, I thank You for Your faithfulness. You have never failed me, and I know that You never will. You have been my provider, my protector, my healer, and my deliverer. I am grateful for the ways You have led me in the past, and I trust that You will continue to lead me in the future.

Thank You for the promises You have made to me, promises that are "yes" and "amen" in Christ Jesus. Thank You for the hope that I have in You, a hope that does not disappoint. Thank You for the new life I have in Christ, a life that is abundant and full of purpose. As I move forward, I do so with a heart full of gratitude, knowing that every good and perfect gift comes from You. I praise You for who You are, for all that You have done, and for all that You will do in my life.

Lord, I dedicate myself to moving forward with You, to never turning back, and to trusting in Your perfect plan for my life. I commit to walking in faith, to living in obedience, and to following wherever You lead. I trust that You are with me every step of the way, and that Your love will sustain me, your grace will empower me, and Your Spirit will guide me. May my life be a testimony to Your faithfulness, and may I always remember that with You, there is no turning back. I will press on toward the goal, to win the prize for which You have called me heavenward in Christ Jesus. I will move forward, not in my own strength, but in the power of Your Spirit, knowing that You are with me, guiding me, and leading me into the abundant life You have promised.

In Jesus' name, I pray.

Amen.

Chapter Eleven
Psalm 23

When David wrote Psalm 23, he was expressing his deep trust and confidence in God as his shepherd and protector. David, who had been a shepherd himself in his youth, used imagery from his experience to convey the care, guidance, and protection God provides to His people. "The Lord is my shepherd; I shall not want."

David is identifying God as a shepherd, someone who cares for, protects, and guides his sheep. The phrase "I shall not want" signifies that with God, he lacks nothing. God provides for all his needs both spiritual and physical. "He makes me lie down in green pastures. He leads me beside still waters. He restores my soul. He leads me in paths of righteousness for His name's sake."

David acknowledges God as the one who provides peace and rest, symbolized by "green pastures" and "still waters." God leads him to places of refreshment and restoration. The "paths of righteousness" signify God's guidance in living a moral, upright life, not for David's glory but for God's. "Yea, though I walk through the valley of the shadow of death, I will fear no evil, for You are with me; Your rod and Your staff, they comfort me."

Here, David reflects on God's presence and protection even in the darkest, most dangerous moments of life. The "valley of the shadow of death" symbolizes severe trials, and yet, David declares he won't be afraid because he knows God is with him. The "rod and staff" represent God's tools of protection and guidance, giving him comfort and security. "You prepare a table before me in the presence of my enemies. You anoint my head with oil; my cup overflows."

Despite adversity (symbolized by enemies), God blesses David abundantly, symbolized by the table, the anointing oil, and the overflowing cup. These images reflect God's favor, abundance, and honor upon David's life, even when he faces opposition. "Surely goodness and mercy shall follow me all the days of my life, and I will dwell in the house of the Lord forever."

David concludes the psalm with a declaration of his unwavering trust in God's goodness and mercy. He is confident that God's love and protection will stay with him throughout his life, and he expresses his desire to be in God's presence forever, whether in this life or in eternity. David was expressing his profound trust in God as a shepherd who leads, provides, protects, and blesses him, even in the most difficult circumstances. The psalm reflects David's personal relationship with God and his assurance that God is with him always, guiding him through life's journey. Walking through darkness can feel like an endless journey. Every step seems uncertain, every breath heavy with the weight of the unknown. In the depths of this tunnel, you're often left to grapple with feelings of isolation, doubt, and fear. The shadows around you may whisper lies—telling you that this journey will never end, that the light you're seeking doesn't exist, or that you're not strong enough to make it.

But the truth is, even in the darkest moments, there's a glimmer of hope. Sometimes, it's faint, almost imperceptible, like a star on a cloudy night. Yet, it's there, waiting for you to take another step forward. The tunnel may twist and turn, and you may stumble or fall, but with every movement, you edge closer to the light. Trusting God when we can't trace Him is one of the deepest acts of faith. It means believing in His goodness, wisdom, and purpose, even when His presence feels distant, and His plan seems unclear. In those moments of uncertainty, when life's circumstances cloud our vision, we're called to lean not on our understanding but to trust that God is still working behind the scenes. Though we may not see Him or understand His ways, faith reminds us that He is always with us, guiding us through the storms and valleys. Trusting God in the unseen is about surrendering control, knowing that His love for us is unwavering, His timing is perfect, and His promises are true. Even in silence, He is near—faithful to lead us to the light, giving us strength for each step.

The search for that light requires faith. Not necessarily faith in immediate answers or clarity, but faith that this struggle is not in vain. It's about trusting that the darkness is temporary, that it's shaping you, refining your strength, and preparing you for what lies ahead. The light at the end of the tunnel is not just a destination; it's a transformation, a place where, after walking through trials, you emerge stronger, more resilient, and deeply connected to your purpose. As you continue your journey, remember that darkness is not your destination. You are a traveler on a path that will lead you to a brighter place. Keep moving forward, step by step, and the light will find you.

A Prayer Acknowledging the Valley & Seeking God's Presence

Heavenly Father,

I come before You today, standing during a valley a place where shadows loom, and the path seems uncertain. Lord, I acknowledge that life sometimes brings moments that feel dark, heavy, and overwhelming. Yet, during this valley, I seek Your presence. I know that You are the God who walks with me, even when I can't fully see Your plan or understand why I am here.

Father, you are my Shepherd, and I trust that You are with me, guiding me with every step I take. Even in this place of uncertainty, where fear and doubt try to overtake me, I hold onto the truth that You will never leave me nor forsake me. Just as David declared, "Yea, though I walk through the valley of the shadow of death, I will fear no evil, for You are with me," I speak those words over my life today.

Lord, help me to be aware of Your presence in this valley. Open my eyes to see that You are here, walking beside me. Remind me that I am not alone, even when the valley feels endless. Strengthen me to trust in Your protection, your wisdom, and Your plan, even when my heart grows weary and the road seems long. Father, I confess that there are times when I try to control my circumstances. I want to know how things will work out, to see the end of the valley before I've walked through it. But today, Lord, I surrender that need for control to You. I give You my fears, my anxieties, and my desire for immediate answers. I trust that You are the One who holds my future in Your hands, and You are guiding me with a purpose far greater than I can comprehend. Teach me, Lord, to release the weight of fear. When my heart is overwhelmed, remind me that You are my rock and my refuge. Help me to rest in the knowledge that You are fighting for me, even when I cannot see it. Though I walk through the valley, I will not fear, because You are with me. You are my protector, my guide, and my strength. Give me the courage to take each step in faith, knowing that You are leading me toward the light at the end of this journey. Help me to lean on Your understanding, not my own, and to trust that even in the valley, you are working all things for my good.

Lord, I know that Your timing is perfect, even when it feels slow to me. In this valley, I sometimes wonder when I will emerge, when I will see the dawn after the darkness. But I surrender my impatience to You, trusting that You know the exact moment when I will reach the other side. I believe that You are using this valley to shape me, to refine my character, and to draw me closer to You.

Help me, Father, to find peace in the waiting. Let my soul rest in the assurance that You are always at work, even in the silence. When I don't hear Your voice, remind me that You are still moving, still working on my behalf. Teach me to wait with hope, to trust in Your wisdom, and to hold onto the promises You have made.

I pray for a heart that is still and quiet before You, that I might hear Your gentle whispers in this valley. When I am tempted to rush ahead or doubt Your plan, remind me that Your ways are higher than mine, and Your thoughts are greater than my own. I trust that You are leading me in paths of righteousness, for Your name's sake, and that this valley is part of the journey You have set before me. Father, I thank You for Your faithfulness. Throughout my life, you have been with me in every season through the highs and the lows, through the valleys and the mountaintops. You have never abandoned me, and I trust that You will not abandon me now. I hold onto the truth that You are the same yesterday, today, and forever. If You have been faithful before, you will be faithful again.

I look to You, Lord, with hope for the future. I believe that this valley is not the end of my story. You are leading me to a place of joy, peace, and abundance on the other side. I trust that as I walk through this valley, you are preparing me for the blessings You have in store. You are strengthening my faith, refining my spirit, and teaching me to depend on You more fully.

As I continue to walk through this season, Lord, I ask that You fill my heart with hope. Let Your peace guard my mind and spirit, and let Your love be my constant companion. Help me to trust that even though I cannot trace every step, you are lighting the way. And when I emerge from this valley, may I look back and see how You carried me, how You worked all things for my good, and how You never left my side. Thank You, Lord, for being my Shepherd, my guide, and my source of strength. I trust you, even in the valley, and I believe that the light of Your presence will lead me through.

In Jesus' name, I pray,

Amen.

Chapter Twelve
Be Still and Know

In the fast-paced world we live in, being still seems almost counterintuitive. We are conditioned to believe that we must always be moving, striving, and doing more to achieve greatness in life. Yet, God calls us to something radically different: to be still and let Him lead. This act of stillness is not passive or weak, but a profound act of faith, trust, and surrender. When we are still, we are acknowledging that we do not hold the reins of our life. We are letting go of the need to control every outcome, every step, and every decision. It is an act of humility, where we admit that our understanding is limited and our vision imperfect. To be still is to recognize that God's plan is far greater and His wisdom infinitely deeper than ours. It is a surrender to His timing, His will, and His direction.

Psalm 46:10 reminds us, "Be still, and know that I am God." This simple yet powerful command invites us into a place of peace, where we no longer strive in our own strength. Instead, we lean into the arms of a loving Father who knows the beginning from the end, who has already mapped out our journey. Stillness is an act of trust it's allowing God to take the lead and guide our lives toward greatness, according to His purpose and plan. Being still also means trusting in God's perfect timing. We often rush through life, impatiently pushing for the next goal, the next achievement, or the next breakthrough. But when we are still, we understand that God's timing is impeccable. He knows when we are ready for the next step, and He knows the seasons of our lives better than we ever could.

In our stillness, we learn to wait on the Lord. Isaiah 40:31 teaches us that "those who wait on the Lord shall renew their strength; they shall mount up with wings like eagles, they shall run and not be weary, they shall walk and not faint." There is strength in waiting strength that comes from knowing that God is preparing us for greatness, even when it seems like nothing is happening. In the waiting, God is at work. He is refining us, molding our character, and aligning circumstances for our good. It's in those moments of stillness that God prepares our hearts for the greatness He has planned. Instead of rushing ahead, we learn to trust that His timing is perfect, and when the time is right, He will open the doors we are meant to walk through. Being still and letting God lead our lives requires us to release fear and anxiety. We often try to control our circumstances out of fear—fear of failure, fear of the unknown, fear that things won't work out as we hope. But when we are still, we are reminded that God is in control. He is the One who holds our future, and His plans for us are filled with hope and purpose. Philippians 4:6-7 encourages us, "Do not be anxious about anything, but in every situation, by prayer and petition, with thanksgiving, present your requests to God. And the peace of God, which transcends all understanding, will guard your hearts and your minds in Christ Jesus." Being still allows us to let go of anxiety and trust that God's peace will guard our hearts as we follow His lead.

When we surrender our fears to God, we are no longer burdened by the weight of trying to make things happen on our own. We trust that He will lead us into the greatness He has designed for us. His plans are not only good but far greater than anything we could ever imagine for ourselves. As we quiet our spirits and trust Him, we find peace that surpasses all understanding, knowing that God's hands are guiding our path. When we are still and allow God to take the lead in our lives, we are positioning ourselves to walk into the greatness He has planned. God's greatness is not defined by worldly standards it is not always about fame, fortune, or success in the eyes of others. Rather, it is about living a life of purpose, walking in alignment with His will, and fulfilling the unique calling He has placed on our lives.

Jeremiah 29:11 speaks of this greatness: "For I know the plans I have for you, declares the Lord, plans to prosper you and not to harm you, plans to give you hope and a future." God's plans for us are good, full of promise and purpose. When I became still and allowed Him to lead, I align myself with these plans. I no longer chase after the things the world tells me I need to be great, but instead, I allow God to shape my destiny according to His design. True greatness comes from a life surrendered to God. It is a life marked by trust, obedience, and faith. As I let go of my own desires and plans, I open myself up to the incredible things God has in store. In His time and in His way, He will lead me into the fullness of His purpose, into a life of significance that reflects His glory. So, Lord, I choose to be still before You today. I lay down my fears, my strife and my need for control. I trust that You are leading me into greatness, not by my might, but by Your Spirit. As I wait on You, I believe that You are preparing me for more than I could ever ask for or imagine. Let my life reflect Your greatness, as I follow You faithfully, step by step, into the future You have prepared.

A Prayer for Seeking Stillness in God's Presence

Heavenly Father,

I come before You today, seeking the peace that only You can provide. My life can often feel chaotic and overwhelming, filled with responsibilities, distractions, and noise. During it all, I find myself longing for stillness a stillness that draws me closer to You, that allows me to rest in Your presence without fear, anxiety, or striving.

Lord, I know that being still before You is not just about physical quiet, but about an inner calm, a surrender of my heart and mind to Your will. As I enter this moment of prayer, I ask that You quiet my spirit. Help me to release everything that is pulling at my attention my worries, my concerns, my fears, and my plans for tomorrow. I lay them all at Your feet, trusting that You are in control of every detail of my life.

You are the God who invites me to be still and know that You are God. I desire to know You more deeply, to experience Your peace during life's storms, and to find refuge in Your presence. As I quiet my heart before You, I ask that You reveal more of Yourself to me. Let Your presence surrounds me, comfort me, and remind me that I am never alone

Father, I confess that there are times when I struggle to be still. My mind races with thoughts of what I need to do, what I should have done, and what might happen in the future. I often try to take control of my life, thinking that I need to figure everything out on my own. But today, I choose to surrender that control to You. I acknowledge that You are the One who holds my life in Your hands, and I trust that Your plans for me are good.

Teach me, Lord, to rest in the knowledge that You are sovereign over all things. You see the beginning and the end, and nothing is hidden from Your sight. Help me to trust that even when I cannot see the way forward, you are guiding me with love and wisdom. Your Word says in Psalm 37:7, "Be still before the Lord and wait patiently for Him." Give me the patience and the faith to wait on You, knowing that Your timing is perfect.

As I release my need for control, I ask that You replace it with a deep sense of peace. Remind me that I don't have to have all the answers, because You do. I don't have to carry the weight of the world on my

shoulders, because You are my strength. In my stillness, I find freedom, because I know that You are working all things together for my good.
Lord, you are my peace. In a world filled with uncertainty and unrest, I find my refuge in You. When the storms of life rage around me, you are my anchor. When the noise of the world drowns out my thoughts, your voice speaks to my heart with clarity and truth. As I sit still before You now, I ask for a greater awareness of Your presence.
Your Word promises in Psalm 46:10, "Be still, and know that I am God." In the stillness, I recognize Your power and majesty. You are the Creator of the universe, the One who holds all things together. And yet, you are also my loving Father, who knows the deepest desires of my heart and cares for every detail of my life. In Your presence, I find rest for my soul.
Lord, help me to cultivate stillness in my daily life. When I am tempted to rush ahead, remind me to pause and seek Your guidance. When I feel overwhelmed, let me turn to You for comfort. And when I am anxious about the future, help me to trust in Your perfect plan. In stillness, I find strength, because I know that You are with me, leading me every step of the way. Father, I believe that in stillness, you are preparing my heart for something greater. As I wait on You, you are shaping my character, deepening my faith, and drawing me closer to Your will. In the still moments, you refine me, teaching me to rely not on my own understanding, but on Your wisdom and grace.
Help me to embrace stillness as a gift a time to connect with You, to reflect on Your goodness, and to rest in the assurance that You are working behind the scenes. I believe that as I continue to seek stillness before You, you will lead me into the fullness of the life You have planned for me. Your Word tells me in Exodus 14:14, "The Lord will fight for you; you need only to be still." In stillness, I surrender my battles to You, trusting that You are fighting for me, making a way where there seems to be no way.
I thank You, Lord, for the peace that comes from being still in Your presence. I thank You for the strength You provide as I rest in You. And I thank You for the greatness You are leading me into, not by my striving, but by Your grace. As I continue to be still before You, I trust that You will guide my life according to Your perfect will.
In Jesus' name, I pray,
Amen.

Chapter Thirteen
Silence
(Who Do I Turn To)

Life can sometimes feel overwhelming, especially during seasons when it seems as though the world is against you. There are moments when every door seems to close, every support system feels fragile, and the people around you seem distant or even antagonistic. It is in these times of hardship, rejection, or misunderstanding that we feel the most vulnerable, searching desperately for solace or understanding.
But what happens when, in the midst of this, God seems silent? When we cry out in prayer, but the answers don't come, when we seek His presence but feel no response, we can begin to question where to turn. This silence can feel like a heavy weight on our hearts, making an already difficult situation feel impossible. It's as though both heaven and earth have conspired against us.

Yet, even in these moments of isolation, there is hope. Though it may feel like God is silent, the truth is that He is still with us. Silence does not mean absence. In fact, the moments when we feel most alone are often when God is closest, working in ways we cannot yet perceive. Even when the world feels against us and God's voice seems distant, He is still our refuge. When it feels like everything is falling apart and God is silent, our natural inclination might be to question, doubt, or even pull away from Him. But these are the moments when faith becomes most crucial. Faith is not just about believing when everything is clear and comfortable; it is about trusting God even when the path is unclear, and His voice is silent.

Throughout the Bible, we see examples of faithful people who faced overwhelming circumstances and felt abandoned by God. Job, for instance, lost everything his family, his wealth, his health and yet, despite God's silence, Job continued to turn to Him. He didn't understand why he was suffering, and he didn't get immediate answers, but he trusted that God was still present, even in the silence.
In times like these, we must remember that God's silence does not indicate His absence or indifference. Sometimes, He uses silence to grow our faith, to teach us endurance, or to guide us into deeper dependence on Him. God may be silent, but He is still our refuge.

When the world is against us, He is the One we must continue to turn to, believing that He hears us, even when we cannot hear Him. In times when God seems silent, His Word remains a powerful source of comfort and guidance. The Bible is filled with promises that remind us of God's unwavering presence and faithfulness, even when our circumstances suggest otherwise. When the world feels hostile, and God's voice seems distant, we can turn to His Word for reassurance. Psalm 34:18 tells us, "The Lord is close to the brokenhearted and saves those who are crushed in spirit." Even when we don't feel it, God is near to us in our pain and brokenness. His silence does not mean He has left us; rather, He is with us in the valley, guiding us through. In these moments, we must cling to the truth of Scripture, trusting that His promises are true, regardless of how we feel.

Isaiah 41:10 also provides reassurance: "So do not fear, for I am with you; do not be dismayed, for I am your God. I will strengthen you and help you; I will uphold you with my righteous right hand." This is a promise that, even when it feels like the world is against us, God is still upholding us. His strength is made perfect in our weakness, and His presence is steadfast, even when we cannot hear His voice.
When God seems silent, we can also find comfort in the lives of others who have experienced the same. Jesus Himself, on the cross, cried out, "My God, my God, why have You forsaken me?" (Matthew 27:46). Even the Son of God experienced a moment of feeling abandoned, yet He remained faithful. In His silence, God is often drawing us closer to His heart, teaching us to rely on His promises rather than our emotions or circumstances. When the world feels like it is against us, and God's voice is hard to hear, we must remember that He is always working behind the scenes. His silence may be part of a larger plan that we cannot yet see. Our job in these moments is to trust Him, even when it feels impossible.

Proverbs 3:5-6 encourages us, "Trust in the Lord with all your heart and lean not on your own understanding; in all your ways submit to Him, and He will make your paths straight." Our understanding is limited, but God's is infinite. His plans for us are good, even when we cannot see them. His silence may be shaping us for something greater, refining our faith, or preparing us for a breakthrough.
In these difficult seasons, we must also surround ourselves with reminders of His goodness. Whether through prayer, worship, or fellowship with other believers, we can keep our hearts focused on His

faithfulness. God's silence is not a sign of abandonment; it is an invitation to deeper trust, to lean into His strength and wait for His perfect timing.

Ultimately, when the world is against us and God seems silent, He is still the one we turn to. He is still our refuge, our strength, and our hope. In the silence, we learn to trust more deeply, to wait more patiently, and to believe that He is working all things for our good. Even when we cannot trace His hand, we trust His heart, knowing that He is with us, carrying us through the storm and leading us into His perfect plan. In those moments of darkness and silence, God is not absent he is present, loving, and faithful. And in His time, His voice will break through the silence, guiding us once again into the light. Until then, we turn to Him, knowing that He is the One who sustains us, even when the world seems to be against us.

A Prayer for Trusting God's Plan When Silence Prevails

Heavenly Father,

I come before You today with a heart that feels heavy and confused. There are times in my life, like now, when I feel like I am crying out to You, but I cannot hear Your voice. It's a difficult place to be, Lord, and my soul longs for Your presence. I know in my heart that You are always with me, but when You seem silent, it's hard to hold on to that truth. I feel lost, unsure of where to go, and unsure of who to turn to. But Lord, I still turn to You, even in this silence.

I ask You, Father, to meet me here in the quiet. I know that silence doesn't mean You have abandoned me or stopped loving me. I believe that You are here, even when I can't feel Your presence. In these moments when You seem distant, help me to draw nearer to You in faith. Help me to remember that You are the same God yesterday, today, and forever. Even when I can't hear Your voice, I trust that You are listening to mine.

Lord, give me the strength to wait on You. When I don't understand what You are doing, and when Your voice feels far away, help me to rest in the knowledge that You are still working. Even in Your silence, you are with me. Teach me to be still in Your presence, trusting that You will speak in Your time. Father, I confess that in this silence, I feel tempted to run to other things—distractions, my own understanding, or even other people for the answers that only You can provide. But I know that these things won't satisfy me. They won't give me the peace that I am searching for. Only You, Lord, can calm the storm in my heart. Only You can provide the guidance and assurance that I need. So even though it is hard, I choose to wait on You.

Help me to trust that Your silence is not a punishment, nor is it an indication that You have left me. I know that sometimes You are silent because You are teaching me something or preparing me for something greater. I believe that You have a plan for my life, a plan that is good and perfect, even when I can't see it. Help me to trust in that plan, Lord.

In the stillness, I ask that You give me the patience to wait on Your timing. I don't want to rush ahead of You or try to solve things on my own. I want to follow where You lead, even if that means walking through this season of silence. I know that You are with me, even when I can't see the way forward. Lord, when You are silent, help me to run to Your Word. Your promises are true, and they are my anchor in the midst of the storm. When I feel like I can't hear Your voice, I can still find Your guidance and comfort in the Bible. Your Word reminds me that You are always with me, that You will never leave me nor forsake me. I know that even in silence, I can rely on the truth of Scripture to guide me and sustain me.

Father, I also pray that You give me the strength to keep coming to You in prayer, even when it feels like You are far away. It's easy to get discouraged when I don't hear Your voice right away, but I know that You hear every prayer I offer. You are not a distant God; You are my loving Father, and You care deeply about every detail of my life. So, I will continue to pray, trusting that You are listening, even when I don't hear You speak back.

Your Word says in Isaiah 40:31, "But those who wait on the Lord shall renew their strength; they shall mount up with wings like eagles, they shall run and not be weary, they shall walk and not faint." I hold on to this promise, Lord. I believe that as I wait on You, you are renewing my strength, even in this silence. You are preparing me for what's ahead, and You are giving me the endurance to keep going.

Lord, I don't want to run to anything or anyone else for what only You can provide. When You seem silent, it's tempting to look for comfort and answers elsewhere, but I know that nothing can fill the space in my heart that belongs to You. I choose to run to You, Lord, even when I don't understand why You are silent. I choose to trust in Your goodness, Your faithfulness, and Your love for me.

In the stillness, remind me that You are working in ways I cannot see. Your silence is not a sign of abandonment; it is often a sign that You are doing something deeper within me. Help me to embrace this season of waiting as a time to grow closer to You, even when I can't hear Your voice. Teach me to trust that You are always present, always working, and always loving me, even when I don't understand Your ways.

Lord, when the world feels heavy, when the burdens I carry seem too much, and when You seem silent, I choose to run to You. You are my refuge, my strength, and my hope. I trust that in Your perfect timing, you will speak. Until then, I will be still before You, trusting in Your presence and Your promises. Thank You for being the God who never leaves me, even in the silence. I trust you, Lord.

In Jesus' name, I pray.

Amen.

Chapter Fourteen
Conversation with God: From Brokenness to Divine Purpose

Life has a way of knocking us down when we least expect it. We struggle through hardships, heartbreaks, disappointments, and loss, often questioning why we face such trials. In those darkest moments, it can feel like the weight of the world is on our shoulders, crushing us under its burden. But amidst the pain, we also find strength, perseverance, and faith. We learn how to stand back up, often stronger than before. For me, this journey has been about having honest conversations with God pouring out my fears, frustrations, and doubts only to find that in releasing my heart, mind, body, and soul, I have unlocked the path to my divine purpose.

"God, why me?" This is a question I have asked countless times during my life. Life has knocked me down in more ways than I can count—whether it was the loss of a loved one, financial struggles, betrayals, or the many internal battles of self-doubt and fear. Each trial felt like a personal attack, as though I was being punished or left to suffer without reason. There were days when I could barely pray, my heart so heavy that words escaped me. Instead, my prayers came in the form of silent tears, a broken spirit reaching out for comfort. "God, where are You in all of this?" I would cry. "Why do I have to endure so much pain? What did I do to deserve this?"

In the depths of my pain, I felt alone. But slowly, through my questions and moments of doubt, I began to realize that God was still there. He hadn't left me, even though I had been too consumed by pain to recognize His presence. This was the beginning of my conversation with God—the raw, honest, sometimes messy expression of my frustrations, anger, and sorrow. I didn't try to mask my feelings or pretend everything was okay. I came to God as I was broken, confused, and weary. God invites us to come as we are, to cast our burdens upon Him because He cares for us (1 Peter 5:7). I learned that God wasn't asking for polished prayers or perfect faith. He wanted my authenticity. He wanted to hear my pain, my struggles, and even my doubts. And in those vulnerable moments of conversation with God, I found the first glimmer of healing. It was in my brokenness that I began to understand that God was never absent; He was right there, waiting for me to surrender everything to Him.

As my relationship with God deepened, so did my understanding of life's challenges. I came to realize that my struggles weren't punishments but were molding me into a stronger, more resilient person. With each hardship, God was teaching me endurance, patience, and trust. This didn't make the challenges any less difficult, but it shifted my perspective. Instead of asking "Why me?" I began to ask, "What can I learn from this, God? How are You using this situation to strengthen me for the future?"

Through each trial, I found myself growing stronger—not because I was immune to pain but because I was learning to lean on God. When I was weak, He became my strength. When I was overwhelmed, He became my peace. When I felt lost, He became my guide. One of the hardest challenges I faced was learning to trust in God's timing. So often, I wanted solutions immediately. I wanted the pain to stop, the situation to change, or the breakthrough to come. But God's timing is different from ours. He sees the bigger picture, while we are often fixated on our immediate needs. It took time, but I began to understand that delays didn't mean denials. God was working behind the scenes, orchestrating things in ways I couldn't yet comprehend.

Overcoming challenges wasn't about eliminating problems or avoiding pain. It was about embracing the process and trusting that God was with me in every step. It was about learning that even when life knocked me down, I had the strength to rise again—not in my own power, but through God's grace. The most profound shift in my life came when I realized that true healing and peace would only come when I surrendered everything to God. For years, I tried to handle things on my own. I tried to control situations, fix problems, and carry the weight of the world on my own shoulders. But it was exhausting, and it left me feeling depleted, anxious, and lost.

"God, I can't do this on my own anymore," I prayed one night, with tears streaming down my face. "I surrender everything to You. My heart, my mind, my body, my soul—take it all, because I can't carry this weight anymore." That prayer of surrender was a turning point. It wasn't a one-time act, but a daily decision to release control and allow

God to lead. Each day, I chose to trust Him more, to let go of my need for control, and to embrace His plans for my life, even when they didn't align with my own.

When I surrendered my heart to God, I found healing for wounds that I had carried for years. When I surrendered my mind, I found peace that surpassed understanding, even during chaos. When I surrendered my body, I found the strength to live in alignment with God's will, honoring Him in every aspect of my life. And when I surrendered my soul, I found true freedom—the kind that only comes from knowing that I belong to God and that His plans for me are good. Surrendering to God opened the door to my divine purpose. I realized that I was not placed on this earth by accident, nor were the challenges I faced random. Every struggle, every heartbreak, and every triumph were part of God's greater plan for my life.

"God, what is Your purpose for me?" I asked, now confident that He had a unique plan for my life. The answer didn't come all at once, but as I continued to seek Him, He began to reveal it little by little. I learned that my purpose wasn't just about what I could achieve or how successful I could be in worldly terms. My purpose was about serving others, glorifying God in all that I do, and using my gifts to make a difference in the world.

God calls each of us to a purpose that is uniquely ours. For some, it may be in ministry or service, for others, it may be in the arts, education, or business. Whatever the calling, God equips us for the tasks He sets before us. In surrendering to Him, we find that He places desires in our hearts that align with His will. And as we walk in obedience, He guides us toward fulfilling that purpose.
Living out my divine purpose means walking in daily relationship with God, trusting Him to guide my steps, and being willing to take risks when He calls me to. It means letting go of my own plans and embracing His, knowing that His ways are higher than mine.

The conversation I have had with God throughout my life has been filled with questions, tears, moments of doubt, and profound realizations. It has been a journey from brokenness to healing, from control to surrender, and from fear to trust. Through it all, I have learned that life's challenges are not meant to destroy me, but to build me up. They are opportunities for growth, for learning, and for drawing closer to God.

As I continue to release my heart, mind, body, and soul to Him, I find that I am walking in a deeper sense of purpose than I ever imagined. I am no longer defined by my past or limited by my fears. Instead, I am empowered by God's love and grace, ready to live out the divine purpose He has placed on my life. And so, I will continue this conversation with God listening, trusting, and walking in faith. For I know that in Him, I have found my true purpose, my true identity, and my true peace.

A Prayer for New Beginnings & A New Release on Life

Heavenly Father,

As I come before You today, my heart is filled with both gratitude and hope. You are the Author of life, the Creator of all things, and in Your hands lie the power to make all things new. As I stand at the threshold of a new beginning, I surrender my heart, mind, body, and soul to You, trusting in Your divine plan for my life. Father, I recognize that I cannot walk this journey on my own; I need Your guidance, your wisdom, and Your strength to carry me through. Thank You for giving me a fresh start, for allowing me to let go of the past, and for leading me into a future that is filled with promise and purpose. I acknowledge that there have been moments in my life when I have felt stuck—stuck in old habits, old patterns of thinking, and old fears. But today, I declare that I am stepping into the newness that You have prepared for me. I let go of everything that has held me back, and I embrace the freedom that comes from living in Your grace.

Help me to let go of the pain, the disappointments, the mistakes, and the regrets that have weighed me down. I release them into Your hands, trusting that You are the God who heals, redeems, and restores. Your Word tells me that You make all things work together for good for those who love You and are called according to Your purpose (Romans 8:28). Today, I choose to believe in that promise. I choose to believe that nothing from my past can hold me captive because You have set me free. Thank You for releasing me from the chains that once bound me and thank You for giving me the strength to move forward in faith.

I ask for a renewed mind. Your Word tells me to be transformed by the renewing of my mind (Romans 12:2), and so I ask for a fresh perspective on life. Renew my thoughts, Lord, so that they align with Your will. Help me to think thoughts of hope, joy, peace, and purpose. Help me to cast down every thought that exalts itself against the knowledge of You (2 Corinthians 10:5). Replace fear with faith, doubt with trust, and confusion with clarity. I know that with You guiding my thoughts, I can walk confidently into the future You have prepared for me.

Father, I also ask for a heart that is fully surrendered to You. You have given me a new release on life, and I want to live it fully for Your glory. Take my heart, Lord, and mold it into the shape You desire. Soften it where it has been hardened by bitterness or pain. Strengthen it where it has been weakened by fear or insecurity. Fill it with Your love, so that I may love others as You have loved me. Remove anything from my heart that is not of You, and replace it with Your truth, Your grace, and Your compassion. Teach me to love with a pure heart, to forgive as You have forgiven me, and to serve others with humility and joy.

Lord, as I release my heart to You, I also release my body and soul. My body is a temple of the Holy Spirit (1 Corinthians 6:19), and I desire to honor You with how I live and care for it. Help me to live in a way that reflects Your goodness. Strengthen me physically, emotionally, and spiritually so that I may serve You with all that I am. Guide me in making choices that honor the life You have given me. Let my body be a vessel through which Your light shines, and let my soul find rest in You, for You are the Source of all peace.

Father, I know that this new release on life is not just about what I let go of, but also about what I embrace. As I release the past, I also open my arms to receive the new blessings You have in store for me. I ask for the discernment to recognize those blessings, even when they come in unexpected forms. Help me to see Your hand at work in every situation and to remain faithful, even when the path is unclear. I know that You are guiding my steps, and so I trust in Your timing and Your plan for my life.

Lord, I pray for clarity of purpose. You have called me to live a life of meaning, a life that reflects Your glory. Show me the path You want me to take. Reveal to me the gifts and talents You have placed within me and help me to use them to build Your kingdom. Let every decision I make, every step I take, and every word I speak be aligned with the purpose You have for my life. I want to live intentionally, knowing that every moment is an opportunity to serve You and to bring honor to Your name.

Father, as I walk in this new beginning, I ask for Your protection and provision. Cover me with Your wings, Lord. Protect me from the schemes of the enemy and from any distractions that would seek to pull me away from Your will. Provide for me in every area of my life—physically, emotionally, financially, and spiritually. I know that You are my Shepherd, and with You, I lack nothing (Psalm 23:1). Help me to trust in Your provision, even when it seems like there is no way. Remind me that You are the God who makes a way in the wilderness and streams in the desert (Isaiah 43:19). I declare that You are making a way for me in this new season.

Lord, thank You for Your presence in my life. Thank You for never leaving me, even when I felt lost or unworthy. Thank You for Your grace that covers me and Your love that never fails. As I embark on this new journey, I ask that You Walk beside me every step of the way. Let me feel Your presence in the quiet moments and in the storms. Remind me that I am never alone, for You are with me always.

Father, I pray for a spirit of gratitude in this new beginning. Help me to be thankful for every blessing, no matter how small. Teach me to see Your hand in both the trials and the triumphs. Let my heart overflow with gratitude for the new opportunities, new experiences, and new relationships You are bringing into my life. And when challenges arise, remind me that You are using them to grow me, to stretch me, and to prepare me for even greater things.

Finally, Lord, I ask for a spirit of obedience. As I release my life fully to You, help me to be obedient to Your voice. When You call me to step out in faith, give me the courage to do so without hesitation. When You ask me to wait, grant me patience and trust in Your perfect timing. Let my heart be sensitive to Your Spirit, so that I may follow Your leading in all that I do.

In this new beginning, I declare that I am Yours. I trust you with my life, my future, and my dreams. I release everything to You, knowing that in Your hands, all things are made new. Thank You for this new release on life, Lord. Thank You for the fresh start You have given me and thank You for the journey ahead. I walk forward in faith, knowing that You are with me, guiding me, and leading me into my divine purpose.

In Jesus' name, I pray.

Amen.

Chapter Fifteen- After the Pain (Learning to Love Again)

Learning to love again after the pain can be one of the most challenging yet rewarding experiences in life. Within this chapter you will explore how to navigate the treacherous waters of emotional recovery and how to embrace the transformative power of love after enduring deep pain. Pain has a way of seeping into the very core of who we are. When it comes from broken relationships, shattered dreams, or personal betrayal, it affects us deeply. We can feel paralyzed by it, hesitant to trust again, and uncertain of our own worth. Emotional pain often triggers a defense mechanism where we build walls around our hearts, convinced that if we avoid vulnerability, we can avoid future hurt. However, this approach, while seemingly protective, can stifle our ability to love and be loved.

Heartbreak alters the way we view love. After a painful breakup or the loss of a significant relationship, it becomes easy to view love as something dangerous or untrustworthy. We question whether love is worth the risk and whether we have the strength to endure potential future pain. This skepticism can lead to emotional isolation, where we deny ourselves the opportunity to experience love again. But avoiding love doesn't eliminate pain it merely reinforces it by keeping us trapped in a cycle of fear.

Learning to love again begins with acknowledging the depth of the pain and the impact it has had on our lives. This requires emotional honesty and a willingness to face the uncomfortable truths about what went wrong and how it affected us. It is not about blaming ourselves or others but understanding the nature of the wound, so we can heal it. Healing is not a linear process. It is messy, often filled with moments of progress and setbacks. One of the most crucial steps in healing from pain is allowing oneself the time and space to grieve. Whether it is the grief of a lost relationship, a friendship, or a dream, acknowledging the loss is essential. Denying our feelings or rushing through them only serves to prolong the healing process.

Grief is an emotional detox, helping us purge the sadness, anger, and confusion that have built up inside. During this time, self-compassion is

vital. We often berate ourselves for not "moving on" quickly enough, or for still feeling hurt months or even years after the initial wound. However, healing on a deeper level requires patience. We must be gentle with ourselves, recognizing that time is a key element in recovery. Another essential component of healing is rediscovering one's sense of self. Pain often clouds our understanding of who we are. When we experience deep emotional wounds, we can start to believe that we are unlovable or broken beyond repair. Part of the healing process involves separating our pain from our identity.
We are not defined by what happened to us, but rather by how we choose to move forward.

Rediscovering personal passions, reconnecting with friends, or pursuing new hobbies can help rebuild a sense of wholeness. Healing from pain requires remembering that life is still rich with possibilities and that we are more than the hurt we have experienced. Perhaps the most daunting aspect of learning to love again is the issue of trust. Trust, once broken, can be difficult to rebuild. Yet, without trust, love cannot thrive. To love again after experiencing pain means learning how to trust in a new way trusting not just in another person, but in ourselves and in the process of life. Trust does not require us to be naïve or ignore the lessons we have learned. On the contrary, it encourages wisdom. We can enter new relationships with a more discerning heart, aware of potential pitfalls but not allowing fear to dictate our decisions. Learning to trust again means we choose to believe in the goodness of people and in the resilience of our own heart.

Rebuilding trust often begins with small steps. We test the waters of vulnerability, gradually allowing ourselves to be open with others. Over time, these small steps add up, and trust is rebuilt through consistency, honesty, and mutual respect. Learning to trust again is about striking a balance between guarding our hearts and being open to the possibility of connection. Ultimately, love is a choice. After experiencing pain, love may no longer feel like an emotion that sweeps us off our feet. Instead, it becomes a deliberate decision to remain open, to choose connection over isolation, and to let go of fear. Love after the pain is not naïve or idealistic—it is courageous. It recognizes the risks involved yet chooses to embrace the vulnerability of loving again.

We also learn that love takes many forms. Romantic love may be what first comes to mind, but the love we experience with friends, family, and even our communities can be just as healing. By expanding our understanding of love, we allow ourselves to receive and give love in different ways, enriching our lives and our sense of belonging. Learning to love again after the pain is a journey of resilience and transformation. It requires honesty, healing, forgiveness, and trust. Most importantly, it requires the courage to choose love, even after we have experienced its opposite. While the scars of the past may remain, they do not define our future. We can emerge stronger, more compassionate, and more open to the boundless possibilities that love offers. After the pain, love is still there waiting for us to embrace it once more.

A Prayer for Learning to Love Again After the Pain

Heavenly Father,

I come before You today with a heart that has been through much. I have endured the pain of love lost, of betrayal, of shattered dreams, and of relationships that left me feeling broken and unsure of myself. Yet, here I am, Lord, standing in Your presence because I know you are the Healer of hearts. I know you are the God who restores, who mends what has been torn apart, and who breathes new life into the places where hope has been lost. Today, Father, I offer You my brokenness and ask You to teach me to love again, even after the pain.

Lord, you know my heart better than I do. You know the wounds that linger, the scars that remain, and the fears that have taken root in me. You see the places where trust has been shattered, where I have closed myself off to protect what remains. Father, I admit that I have been afraid to love again. I have been afraid of the vulnerability, the potential for more hurt, and the unknowns that come with opening my heart to someone else. But I know, deep down, that You have not called me to live in fear. You have called me to love—fully, freely, and without reservation.

So, Father, I ask for Your healing touch to mend the broken places in my heart. Heal the wounds that have come from the past, the disappointments, the betrayals, and the losses that have caused me to question whether I can love again. I lay these hurts at Your feet, Lord, trusting that You will take them and transform them into something beautiful. Your Word tells me that You are close to the brokenhearted and that You save those who are crushed in spirit (Psalm 34:18). I hold onto that promise today, believing that You are not only near to me in this season but that You are actively working to restore my heart.

Father, as You heal my heart, teach me to trust again. Trust is such a delicate thing, and I admit that it feels fragile after what I have been through. It feels risky to open my heart again and to trust someone with the most vulnerable parts of who I am. But I know that true love requires trust. So, Lord, I ask that You help me to rebuild my trust, first and foremost, in You. Help me to remember that You are trustworthy, that You never fail, and that You hold all things in Your hands. When I struggle to trust others, remind me that my ultimate trust is in You.

Even if people fail me, You never will.

Teach me to trust in Your timing, Lord. Teach me to trust that You know what is best for me and that You are guiding my steps. Help me to trust that You have a plan for my life that is good and that includes love. Your Word says that You withhold no good thing from those who walk uprightly (Psalm 84:11), and so I trust that You will not withhold the good gift of love from me. When I am tempted to rush ahead or to settle for less than what You desire for me, remind me to wait on You. Help me to be patient, knowing that Your timing is perfect, and that You are preparing my heart and the heart of the one You have for me.

Lord, I ask for wisdom in learning to love again. Give me discernment in my relationships. Help me to see people as You see them, not through the lens of my past pain, but through the lens of grace and truth. Teach me to recognize the qualities that reflect Your heart in others and to pursue relationships that honor You. Protect me from falling into patterns of hurt or unhealthy dynamics and guide me toward the kind of love that mirrors Your love—selfless, patient, and kind. Let me be wise in who I give my heart to but let me not be so guarded that I close myself off to the possibility of genuine love.

Father, I also ask for the courage to be vulnerable again. Love requires vulnerability, and that is something that can feel so difficult after experiencing pain. It can feel safer to build walls, to protect myself from ever getting hurt again, but I know that love cannot flourish behind walls. Love requires openness and honesty. It requires the willingness to share my heart, my fears, and my dreams with someone else. So, I ask for the courage to be vulnerable, not just with others, but also with You, Lord. Help me to bring my fears and insecurities to You, trusting that You can transform them into strength and confidence. And when the time comes, help me to be open with others, trusting that love is worth the risk.

Lord, remind me that love is a gift from You. Sometimes I forget that love is not something I need to earn or chase after. It is a gift that You have created, a reflection of Your very nature. Your Word tells me that You are love (1 John 4:8) and that all love comes from You. Teach me to receive love as a gift from Your hand. Help me to rest in the knowledge that I am already fully and deeply loved by You, and that no human love can ever take the place of the love You have for me. Let that truth be the foundation upon which I build any future relationship. Let me seek love not from a place of lack or desperation, but from a place of wholeness, knowing that I am already complete in You.

Father, I also pray for forgiveness—both for myself and for others. I know that in order to love again, I must be willing to forgive those who have hurt me in the past. I release them into Your hands, Lord, choosing to forgive them just as You have forgiven me. I choose to let go of any bitterness, anger, or resentment that has lingered in my heart. I also ask for forgiveness for the times when I have hurt others, knowingly or unknowingly. Cleanse my heart, Lord, and make it pure. As I forgive and release the past, I ask that You fill my heart with Your peace and Your love, preparing me for the new relationships You have in store. Lord, as I learn to love again, I ask for grace. Grace for myself, grace for others, and grace for the process of healing and growth. I know that love is not always easy, and there will be times when I stumble or make mistakes. But I trust that Your grace is sufficient for me, and that You will guide me through every step of this journey. Help me to extend grace to myself when I am tempted to be hard on myself or when I feel like I'm not progressing fast enough. And help me to extend grace to others, knowing that no one is perfect, but that we are all works in progress.

Heavenly Father, as I move forward, I ask that You fill my heart with hope. Hope for the future, hope for new beginnings, and hope for the love that is to come. Let me not dwell in the pain of the past but let me look forward with anticipation to the new things You are doing in my life. Your Word says that You are doing a new thing, making a way in the wilderness and streams in the desert (Isaiah 43:19). I believe that You are making a way for me, Lord, and I trust that this new chapter will be filled with love, joy, and peace. Let me walk forward in faith, knowing that You are guiding my steps and that Your plans for me are good.

Finally, Lord, I ask that You teach me to love as You love.

Let my love be patient and kind, not envious or boastful, not arrogant or rude. Let my love be selfless and forgiving, bearing all things, believing all things, hoping all things, and enduring all things (1 Corinthians 13:4-7). Teach me to love in a way that reflects Your heart, and let that love be a testimony of Your goodness and grace in my life.

Thank You, Lord, for this journey of learning to love again. Thank You for Your healing, Your guidance, and Your faithfulness. I trust you with my heart, and I trust that in Your perfect timing, you will bring the right people into my life. Until then, I will rest in Your love, knowing that it is more than enough for me.

In Jesus' name, I pray.

Amen.

Chapter Sixteen
Greater is Coming: Finding Joy after the Storm

Life is full of seasons—some filled with joy and others with pain. We all encounter trials and tribulations that test our faith and strength. There are moments when it seems like the storms of life will never end. Yet, for those who trust in God, there is always a promise that greater is coming. Trouble doesn't last always. The rain may pour, the winds may rage, and the fires may burn, but in the end, there is sunshine and a rainbow waiting on the other side. This chapter explores the journey through life's storms, the faith that sustains us through those trials, and the joy and peace that await when we come out stronger and wiser. Storms in life are inevitable. No one is exempt from hardship. Whether it's financial struggles, broken relationships, loss, or personal battles, storms often come when we least expect them. In these moments, the weight of our circumstances can feel overwhelming. We may cry out to God, asking why we have to endure such pain. The dark clouds seem endless, and it's easy to lose sight of hope.

In the midst of the storm, it can feel as if God is far away, but He is always present. Psalm 34:19 reminds us, "Many are the afflictions of the righteous, but the Lord delivers him out of them all." This means that while we will face difficulties, we are never alone. God walks with us through every trial, providing strength and comfort even when we feel weak. Storms often come to shake us and to test the foundation of our faith. They strip away the things we hold dear and force us to confront our vulnerabilities. But these storms are not sent to destroy us; rather, they are allowed by God to build something greater within us. Like a tree that grows stronger after surviving a fierce wind, our faith is fortified through every storm we endure. We may bend, but we do not break because God's hand is upon us.

The rain in our lives can symbolize the moments of sadness, grief, and uncertainty. When we are caught in the downpour, it can feel endless, as though the sun will never shine again. But rain has a purpose. It nourishes the earth and helps things grow. Similarly, the trials we face can water our spirits, growing our faith and endurance. James 1:2-4 tells us to "consider it pure joy whenever you face trials of many kinds, because you know that the testing of your faith produces perseverance." Even in the rain, God is at work, preparing us for something greater.

Beyond the rain, there are times when we must walk through the fire. The fire represents those intense moments of life where the pressure is unbearable, and we feel as though we are being refined. Just as gold is purified in fire, so too are we purified through the hardships we face. In Isaiah 43:2, God says, "When you walk through the fire, you will not be burned; the flames will not set you ablaze." This promise reminds us that while the fire may be hot, it will not consume us. God uses the fire to refine us, removing impurities and making us stronger and wiser.
In the heat of the fire, it's difficult to see how anything good can come from our suffering. But it is often through these fiery trials that God reveals His greatest blessings. As we endure, our faith becomes stronger, our character is developed, and we learn to trust God in deeper ways. The fire may be painful, but it is necessary for the growth and transformation that God desires for our lives.

After enduring the storm, the rain, and the fire, we emerge on the other side not as the same person but as someone stronger, wiser, and more resilient. Every trial we face teaches us something new about ourselves and about God. We learn that we are capable of enduring more than we ever imagined, and we discover that God's grace is sufficient to carry us through even the darkest times. When we come out of the storm, we have a testimony that can inspire and encourage others. The world needs to hear that there is hope after the storm, that joy comes in the morning, and that trouble truly doesn't last always. Our story of survival becomes a beacon of hope for those still during their trials. We can say with confidence, "I've been through the storm, but I came out stronger, and you can too."

The wisdom gained from our trials allows us to see life from a different perspective. We no longer take the sunshine for granted, and we appreciate the moments of peace and joy that follow the storm. We also recognize the importance of trusting God through every season of life, knowing that He is always working for our good, even when we cannot see it. As Romans 8:28 reminds us, "And we know that in all things God works for the good of those who love him, who have been called according to his purpose." No matter how long the storm lasts, there is always a promise that joy is coming. Psalm 30:5 says, "Weeping may endure for a night, but joy comes in the morning." This verse reminds us that our struggles are temporary, and God's joy is eternal. After the storm passes, we step into a new season of joy and peace that is all the sweeter because of what we've endured.

The rainbow that appears after the storm is a symbol of God's promise and faithfulness. Just as He promised Noah that He would never again flood the earth, God promises us that He will never leave us or forsake us. The rainbow is a reminder that greater is coming. The trials we face are not the end of our story; they are simply the path we must walk to reach the blessings that God has in store for us. Joy is not dependent on our circumstances. It is rooted in the knowledge that God is in control and that He has a purpose for everything we go through. Even in the midst of the storm, we can experience a sense of peace and joy because we know that God is working behind the scenes to bring about something greater. Our joy comes from trusting in His promises and knowing that He will bring us through to the other side.

The storms of life may seem overwhelming, but they are not meant to destroy us. They are meant to refine us, strengthen us, and prepare us for the greater things that God has in store. Though the rain may fall, and the fire may burn, we can stand firm in the knowledge that God is with us every step of the way. Greater is coming, and joy is on the horizon. Trouble doesn't last always, and the sunshine and rainbow that follow the storm are a testament to God's faithfulness and love. As we go through life's trials, let us remember that our struggles are temporary, but the joy that comes from trusting in God is eternal.

A Prayer- Joy Will Come in the Morning

Heavenly Father,

I come before You today with a heart that has weathered many storms. Life has brought challenges, hardships, and trials that have tested my faith, my strength, and my endurance. There have been moments when I felt like the waves of life would overwhelm me, when the darkness of the storm seemed too great to bear. But, Lord, I am still here. I stand in Your presence today because You are faithful. You carried me through the storm, and I know that You will continue to lead me into a place of peace and joy.

Father, as I emerge from this season of trial, I come seeking the joy that only You can provide. The storm has passed, but its effects linger in my heart and mind. There are wounds that need healing, doubts that need comforting, and hopes that need rekindling. Yet, in the midst of it all, I know that You are the source of true joy. I know that my circumstances do not define my joy; rather, my joy comes from knowing and trusting You. So today, Lord, I ask that You help me find joy after the storm.

Lord, I thank You for carrying me through the storm. I acknowledge that it was only by Your grace that I was able to endure the trials that came my way. You were my refuge when the winds of life blew fiercely. You were my anchor when I felt lost and adrift. You were my strength when I had none left to give. Thank You for never leaving my side, even when I couldn't see or feel Your presence. Your Word promises that You will never leave nor forsake me (Deuteronomy 31:6), and I have experienced the truth of that promise firsthand. I am grateful, Lord, for Your sustaining power and for the way You held me together when everything else seemed to fall apart.

Now that the storm has passed, Lord, I ask that You restore my joy. I know that joy is a gift from You, not something that I can create on my own. I also know that joy is not dependent on my external circumstances, but on my relationship with You. So, Father, draw me closer to You in this season. Let my heart be filled with the joy that comes from knowing You intimately and trusting in Your goodness. Help me to find joy in Your presence, for in Your presence is fullness of joy (Psalm 16:11). Let that joy overflow into every area of my life, even as I continue to heal from the effects of the storm.

Father, I ask that You heal my heart. The storms of life often leave us with scars—emotional, mental, and even spiritual wounds that need time to mend. You know the areas of my heart that have been hurt, the places where fear, doubt, and weariness have taken hold. But I believe, Lord, that You are the God who heals. Your Word tells me that You heal the brokenhearted and bind up their wounds (Psalm 147:3), and so I ask for Your healing touch in my life. Remove any lingering pain, bitterness, or discouragement that the storm has left behind. Replace it with Your peace, Your love, and Your joy. Let me not carry the weight of the storm with me into the future but let me be free to embrace the new season of life that You have for me.

Lord, help me to find joy in the small things again. When we go through difficult seasons, it's easy to lose sight of the everyday blessings that surround us. The storm can blind us to the beauty and goodness that still exist in our lives. But, Lord, I know that even in the midst of the storm, you were still at work, providing for me, caring for me, and surrounding me with Your grace. Help me to open my eyes to those blessings now that the storm has passed. Teach me to find joy in the simple things—a sunrise, a kind word, a moment of peace. Remind me that every good and perfect gift comes from You (James 1:17), and that You are constantly pouring out Your love and goodness on me, even in the smallest details of life.

Father, I also ask for the strength to rebuild after the storm. There are parts of my life that may need to be rebuilt—relationships, dreams, and even my faith. But I trust that You are a God of restoration, and that what the storm has broken, you can restore. Help me to approach this season of rebuilding with joy, knowing that You are with me in every step. Let me not be discouraged by the work ahead, but instead be filled with the joy of knowing that You are guiding and empowering me. Your Word says that the joy of the Lord is my strength (Nehemiah 8:10), and so I rely on that joy to give me the strength I need to move forward. I trust that as I rebuild, you will do immeasurably more than I could ever ask or imagine (Ephesians 3:20).

Lord, as I find joy in You, help me to share that joy with others. The storm may have been a time of isolation and inward focus, but now I want to turn outward and share the joy You have given me with those around me. Teach me to be a light in the lives of others, especially those who may still be in the midst of their own storms. Let the joy that I have found in You be a testimony to Your goodness and faithfulness. Use me, Lord, to encourage and uplift others, to remind them that there is hope and joy on the other side of their trials. Let my life be a reflection of Your joy, so that others may be drawn to You.

Father, I pray for joy during uncertainty. Even though the storm has passed, there may still be challenges ahead. Life is unpredictable, and I don't always know what the future holds. But I do know that my joy is not dependent on what happens tomorrow. My joy is found in You, and You are unchanging. So, Lord, help me to remain joyful even when the future is unclear. Help me to trust that You are in control, and that whatever comes, you will be with me. Let my joy be a steady anchor in my life, not swayed by circumstances, but rooted in the unshakable truth of Your love and Your promises.

Father, I thank You for the lessons the storm has taught me. Even though it was difficult, I know that You used the storm to grow me, to refine me, and to draw me closer to You. I thank You for the strength that has been built in me through the trial, for the faith that has been deepened, and for the new perspective I have gained. I ask that You help me to carry these lessons with me as I move forward, and that they would serve as a reminder of Your faithfulness. Let me look back on the storm, not with bitterness, but with gratitude for the ways You worked in and through it.

Lord, I pray for peace as I find joy. Let Your peace guard my heart and mind as I continue to heal and grow. Let Your peace calms any remaining anxieties or fears that may try to resurface. I know that Your peace surpasses all understanding (Philippians 4:7), and I ask that it fill every corner of my heart. Let that peace be the foundation of my joy, knowing that no matter what happens, you are with me, and You are for me.

Heavenly Father, as I close this prayer, I ask for an outpouring of Your joy in my life. Let it flow into every aspect of my being—my thoughts, my emotions, my relationships, and my work. Let it be a joy that is contagious, spreading to those around me and glorifying Your name. Let my life be a testimony of the joy that comes after the storm, a reflection of Your goodness and grace. I thank You, Lord, for the joy that is already mine, and I trust that it will only grow as I continue to walk with You.

In Jesus' name, I pray.

Amen.

Chapter Seventeen
Forever Worship

Life is full of trials, tribulations, and obstacles that often seem insurmountable. At various points in our journey, we encounter situations that threaten to break us, steal our joy, and leave us feeling defeated. But as believers, we know that no challenge is greater than the power and grace of God. It is through the hardest moments that God demonstrates His love and strength, pulling us through what was meant to destroy us. As I reflect on the significance of overcoming life's obstacles, the gratitude that comes from experiencing God's deliverance, and the importance of forever worshipping and glorifying Him for His unending faithfulness.

Each of us has faced moments where the challenges of life seemed overwhelming—whether it was a season of deep emotional pain, financial hardship, physical illness, broken relationships, or spiritual battles. In these dark moments, it's easy to feel as though we've reached the end of ourselves. The weight of the burdens we carry can be so heavy that we wonder if we'll ever rise above them. The Bible tells us that trials are inevitable in this life (John 16:33), but as believers, we understand that these trials are not meant to destroy us. Instead, they refine us and bring us closer to God.

There were moments in my life when it seemed that the obstacles in front of me were specifically designed to break my spirit. It felt as though the enemy had strategically placed roadblocks in my path, with the goal of causing me to doubt my worth, my purpose, and even God's love for me. But even in those moments of despair, a small voice deep within reminded me that God was still with me. I may have felt crushed, but I was never abandoned. Looking back, I realize that what was meant to destroy me was simply a part of the journey that led me to a deeper relationship with God. As I reflect on the trials I've faced, I can clearly see God's hand at work in every situation. It wasn't my strength that carried me through—it was God's grace and power that pulled me out of the pit. The Bible tells us that God's strength is made perfect in our weakness (2 Corinthians 12:9), and I've experienced this truth firsthand. When I had no more energy to fight, no more words to pray, and no more tears to cry, God stepped in. He gave me the strength to endure, the peace to trust His plan, and the faith to believe that He would see me through.

One of the most beautiful aspects of God's grace is that it's freely given, even when we feel undeserving. There were times when I questioned whether God would show up for me because I had made mistakes or doubted Him. But God's love doesn't waver based on our imperfections. His grace is sufficient, and His mercies are new every morning (Lamentations 3:22-23). I am eternally grateful for the ways in which God's grace has sustained me, covered me, and restored me.
It was during the lowest points in my life that I learned the most about God's character. He is not only our Savior but also our Comforter, Provider, Healer, and Deliverer. Every time I thought I couldn't go any further, God reminded me that I was not walking alone. He was there, guiding me through the valley, providing exactly what I needed to overcome each obstacle. Whether it was a financial breakthrough, a restored relationship, or healing from emotional wounds, God proved Himself faithful time and time again. There is something transformative about coming out on the other side of a trial. The gratitude that fills your heart is indescribable.
When I look back at the obstacles I've overcome, I am filled with overwhelming gratitude—not only for the victory but for the journey itself. Every hardship taught me something valuable about myself and, more importantly, about God. I've learned to trust Him in ways I never thought possible, to rely on His Word even when my circumstances seemed impossible, and to find peace in His presence even in the midst of chaos. The obstacles that were meant to destroy me have only strengthened my faith. They have shaped me into the person I am today, and for that, I am forever grateful. I no longer view hardships as a sign of God's absence but as an opportunity for His power to be revealed in my life. James 1:2-4 tells us to consider it pure joy when we face trials of many kinds because the testing of our faith produces perseverance. I now understand that perseverance is a gift, and it is through the fire of trials that we are refined.

Gratitude goes beyond simply saying "thank you." It's a posture of the heart that recognizes that everything we have, everything we've overcome, and everything we are because of God. I am grateful for the times when God said "no" because He had something better. I am grateful for the moments when He allowed me to struggle because it drew me closer to Him. I am grateful for the lessons learned, the strength gained, and the peace that comes from knowing that God is in control. The Bible tells us in 1 Thessalonians 5:18 to give thanks in all circumstances, for this is God's will for us in Christ Jesus. Worship is not just something we do on Sundays; it's a lifestyle. Worship is the response of a grateful heart, and I have learned to worship God not just for what He has done but for who He is. He is worthy of all honor, glory, and praise because He is faithful, loving, and good.

When I think about the obstacles that were placed in my life to destroy me, I can't help but worship God for His deliverance. He is the reason I am still standing, the reason I have peace in my heart, and the reason I can walk in freedom. My worship is a declaration that God is greater than any trial, stronger than any attack of the enemy, and more powerful than any circumstance. God deserves the glory because, without Him, I would not have made it. He fought battles I didn't even know existed, protected me from dangers I couldn't see, and provided for me when I had nothing. Psalm 34:1 says, "I will bless the Lord at all times; His praise shall continually be in my mouth." This verse has become my life's anthem because I will never stop praising the God who pulled me out of the pit and placed me on solid ground.

As I reflect on the obstacles that were placed in my life to destroy me, I can say with confidence that God is the reason I am victorious today. His grace was sufficient, His strength carried me, and His love sustained me. I am forever grateful for the journey, for every lesson learned, and for the ways in which God has shown His faithfulness. Above all, I am committed to forever worshipping and glorifying God for pulling me through the darkest seasons of my life. He deserves all the honor and all the glory, now and forevermore.

A Prayer for Worshipping the True and Living God

Heavenly Father,

I come before You with a heart full of gratitude, awe, and reverence. There is no one like You, Lord—no one who is so holy, so powerful, so merciful, and so loving. You are the Alpha and the Omega, the Beginning and the End. You spoke the universe into existence with a word, and You hold all things together by Your power. And yet, you also know me intimately and love me deeply. How could I not worship You, Lord? How could I not devote every part of my life to honoring and glorifying You?

Father, I offer myself to You in this moment, dedicating my life to a posture of forever worship. I acknowledge that worship is not just a song or a moment, but a lifestyle. It is the constant recognition of who You are and the response of my heart to Your greatness. Worship is surrender. Worship is trust. Worship is a daily, moment-by-moment choice to live for Your glory and not for my own. And so, Lord, today I ask that You teach me to live a life of worship, not just for a season, but for all eternity.

Lord, I worship You for who You are. You are my Creator, the One who knit me together in my mother's womb and knows every hair on my head. You are my Provider, the One who meets all of my needs and sustains me day by day. You are my Healer, the One who restores my soul and makes me whole. You are my Savior, the One who sent Your Son, Jesus Christ, to die on the cross for my sins so that I might have eternal life. You are my Redeemer, the One who takes what was broken and makes it beautiful. You are my Shepherd, the One who leads me beside still waters and restores my soul. You are my King, the One who reigns over all things, and yet You invite me to come boldly before Your throne of grace.

There are no words that can fully capture how worthy You are of my worship, Lord. Your greatness is beyond comprehension. Your love is deeper than the oceans and wider than the sky. You are good, and Your mercy endures forever. You are holy, and there is none like You. And so, Father, I declare today that I will worship You for all of my days, not just with my lips, but with my heart, my mind, and my life. Let every thought, every word, and every action be an offering of worship to You.

Father, I worship You not just for what You do, but for who You are. Yes, you have blessed me beyond measure. Yes, you have been faithful to me in every season of my life. You have provided for me, protected me, and guided me. But even if You had done none of those things, you would still be worthy of my worship simply because of who You are. You are God, and You are good. You are holy, righteous, and just. You are love, peace, and joy. You are everything I could ever need, and more. And so, I worship You, Lord, not for what I can get from You, but because You are worthy of all my praise.

Lord, I ask that You transform my heart into a heart of worship. There are times when my heart is distracted by the things of this world, times when I am consumed by my own worries, desires, or frustrations. But I know, Father, that true worship requires a heart that is fully focused on You. So I ask that You would remove any idols from my life—anything that I have placed above You, whether it be my own plans, relationships, material things, or even my own self. Let my heart be undivided in its devotion to You. Teach me to fix my eyes on You, the Author and Perfecter of my faith (Hebrews 12:2). Let the distractions of this world fade away as I gaze upon Your beauty and glory.

Father, I also ask that You teach me to worship You in spirit and in truth. Your Word says that the kind of worshipers You seek are those who worship in spirit and in truth (John 4:23). I don't want my worship to be just an outward show or an empty ritual. I want it to be genuine, heartfelt, and rooted in the truth of who You are. Help me to worship You from the depths of my being, with all my heart, soul, mind, and strength. Let my worship be anchored in the truth of Your Word, not based on my emotions or circumstances, but on the unchanging reality of who You are. Whether I am on the mountaintop or in the valley, let my worship remain steadfast, for You are always worthy and in all seasons.

Lord, I want to worship You in the everyday moments of life. It's easy to worship You in the grand moments, when I feel Your presence in a powerful way or when I see Your hand moving in my life. But I know that true worship is found in the everyday moments—in the mundane, the ordinary, the unnoticed. So, Father, teach me to worship You in the small things. Help me to see that every moment of my life is an opportunity to offer praise to You. Whether I am working, resting, serving, or simply going about my daily tasks, let it all be done for Your glory. Let my life be a living sacrifice, holy and pleasing to You, for this is my spiritual act of worship (Romans 12:1).

Father, I pray that my worship would reflect Your love. Your love is perfect, pure, and unconditional. It is a love that gave everything for me, a love that sent Your only Son to die in my place so that I might have eternal life. In response to that love, I want my worship to reflect the love You have shown me. Let my worship be marked by love—for You, for others, and for the world around me. Help me to love You with all my heart, soul, mind, and strength, and to love my neighbor as myself (Mark 12:30-31). Let my worship move beyond words and songs and into acts of love, service, and kindness.

Father, I ask that You use my worship to draw others to You. When I live a life of worship, I know that it is a testimony to the world of Your goodness and grace. I ask that You use my worship to be a light in the darkness, to point others to the hope and salvation that is found in You alone. Let my life reflect Your glory, so that others may see You in me and be drawn to worship You as well. Let my worship be contagious, spreading the fragrance of Your love and grace wherever I go.

Lord, I know that worship is not limited to this life. You have created me for eternity, and my worship will continue long after this earthly life has passed. One day, I will stand before You in heaven, surrounded by the angels and saints, and I will worship You forever. I look forward to that day, Lord, when I will see You face to face and worship You in all Your glory. But until that day comes, I will worship You here on earth, with all that I am and all that I have. Let my life be a preparation for the eternal worship that is to come, as I join with all of creation in declaring, "Holy, holy, holy is the Lord God Almighty, who was, and is, and is to come" (Revelation 4:8).

Heavenly Father, I declare today that I will forever worship You. No matter what life brings, no matter what challenges or blessings come my way, I will choose to worship You. I will worship You in the good times and the bad, in the joys and the sorrows, in the abundance and in the lack. For You are worthy of all my praise, all my love, and all my devotion. I offer my life to You as an act of worship, and I ask that You would be glorified in everything I do. Let my worship rise to You like sweet incense, pleasing and acceptable in Your sight.

Thank You, Lord, for the privilege of worshiping You. Thank You for the gift of Your presence, and for the joy that comes from knowing and loving You. I commit myself to a lifetime and an eternity of worship, for You are worthy of it all.

In Jesus' precious name, I pray.

Amen.

Chapter Eighteen
Overcoming a Broken Marriage

Infidelity can be one of the most devastating experiences in a marriage. It breaks trust, shatters dreams, and leaves a trail of emotional devastation that can feel impossible to overcome. For many, the pain caused by such betrayal goes beyond the surface—it cuts deeply into the heart, mind, and soul. Yet, even in the darkest moments, God's grace shines as a beacon of hope, offering a path toward healing and renewal. This essay explores how God's grace can be sufficient for those who endure the heartbreak of infidelity, ultimately leading to a life of freedom, peace, and happiness. When infidelity occurs in a marriage, the impact is profound and far-reaching. Trust, the very foundation of a relationship, is destroyed, leaving both partners feeling broken and disoriented. For the betrayed spouse, the discovery of the affair can lead to feelings of worthlessness, rejection, and shame.

Questions begin to swirl in the mind: "What did I do wrong? Was I not enough? Why wasn't I chosen?" These thoughts often trigger deep emotional wounds that can affect one's sense of identity and self-worth. The mind becomes a battlefield as anger, bitterness, and sadness take root. Memories of the relationship and moments once cherished are now tainted with pain. In addition to the emotional turmoil, infidelity also affects the soul, leaving a deep sense of spiritual abandonment. Many find themselves crying out to God, asking, "Why did this happen to me?" The betrayal can create feelings of isolation from others and from God.

In these moments, the pain can seem overwhelming, and the future may feel uncertain. But it is precisely in these moments of deep sorrow and brokenness that the grace of God begins to work in ways that are beyond human understanding. The journey to healing is not immediate, but it is possible—especially when rooted in God's grace. God's grace is often described as "unmerited favor," a gift freely given by a loving Father to His children. In times of heartache, grace becomes the lifeline that helps us take our first steps toward healing. It is in these moments of surrender, when we realize we cannot heal on our own, that God steps in with His transformative power.

The first step in overcoming a broken marriage due to infidelity is to open one's heart to the grace of God. This means acknowledging the pain, the hurt, and the loss but also recognizing that God's love is bigger than the betrayal. In Matthew 11:28, Jesus says, "Come to me, all you who are weary and burdened, and I will give you rest." These words are a reminder that, in times of distress, God invites us to lay our burdens at His feet. Through prayer and reflection, the betrayed spouse can begin to find solace in the arms of a loving God. This period of seeking God's comfort helps to recalibrate the heart, mind, and soul toward healing. God's grace gently removes the layers of anger and bitterness, replacing them with His peace.

The mind, which was once filled with thoughts of inadequacy and pain, begins to renew itself through God's Word. Passages like Romans 12:2—"Do not conform to the pattern of this world but be transformed by the renewing of your mind"—become essential in reorienting one's thinking. By meditating on God's promises, the heart and mind are slowly restored, making room for healing and forgiveness. Perhaps one of the most challenging aspects of healing from infidelity is the process of forgiveness. It is natural to feel anger and resentment toward the spouse who has betrayed the marriage covenant. Yet, harboring unforgiveness only leads to further emotional and spiritual bondage. The journey to freedom is inextricably linked to the willingness to forgive.

On the road to freedom and true healing, especially after significant emotional pain such as infidelity, trauma, or personal betrayal, there are several key steps that help guide the journey. True healing involves the heart, mind, and soul, and it's important to acknowledge that the process takes time, patience, and God's grace.

Here are the key steps for achieving freedom and healing:

1. Acknowledging the Pain- The first step toward healing is recognizing and accepting the pain you've experienced. Suppressing or ignoring the hurt only prolongs the healing process. It's crucial to allow yourself to grieve the betrayal, loss, or brokenness. Acknowledging your feelings without guilt is an essential part of emotional recovery.

Action: Journaling your emotions or speaking with a trusted friend, therapist, or spiritual counselor can help you express and process the pain.

2. Surrendering to God- Healing often begins when we realize we cannot heal by our own strength. Surrendering the hurt, anger, and bitterness to God is key to allowing His grace to work in your life. God is willing to carry our burdens and bring restoration where we see no hope.

Action: In prayer, ask God for strength and peace, and release control of the situation to Him. Trust His timing and His plan for your healing.

3. Renewing Your Mind- The Bible speaks of the importance of renewing the mind (Romans 12:2). Emotional wounds can create toxic thought patterns that affect how you view yourself, your relationships, and your future. To heal, it's necessary to replace negative, destructive thoughts with God's truth.

Action: Focus on Scriptures that affirm your identity in Christ. Surround yourself with positive, uplifting material that speaks life into your situation. Meditate on verses like Philippians 4:8, which encourages focusing on what is true, noble, and praiseworthy.

4. Choosing Forgiveness- Forgiveness is a vital step in the healing process. Holding onto resentment, anger, and bitterness binds you to the past and prevents true freedom. Forgiving doesn't mean condoning the wrong, but it releases you from the emotional hold the situation has on you. Forgiveness is more about your healing than the other person's actions.

Action: Begin the process of forgiving those who hurt you by asking God for the grace to release them. This may take time, but each step brings you closer to emotional freedom

5. Embracing God's Grace- Healing is not about perfection, but about embracing the grace of God in your brokenness. Grace allows you to be vulnerable before God and others, admitting that you need help to move forward. Grace also empowers you to move beyond guilt and shame and live in the freedom that God offers.

Action: Remember that God's grace is sufficient (2 Corinthians 12:9).

Accept the fact that you don't have to be "strong" or "perfect" all the time. Lean into His grace for every step of the journey.

6. Setting Healthy Boundaries- True healing often requires setting healthy boundaries with people and situations that may trigger past hurts or enable toxic patterns. Boundaries help protect your emotional, mental, and spiritual health as you recover and grow.

Action: Learn to say no to situations and relationships that drain you or pull you back into negative cycles. Surround yourself with supportive, healthy relationships that encourage your healing and growth

7. Seeking Community and Support- Healing is not meant to be done in isolation. The support of a faith community, friends, or a counselor can provide the encouragement and wisdom needed to continue the road to healing. God often works through others to help us in our journey.

Action: Engage with your church, support groups, or counseling resources that align with your values and can offer guidance and love as you heal.

8. Restoring Your Identity in Christ- Infidelity, betrayal, and other forms of brokenness can damage your sense of self. Part of the healing process is rediscovering your worth and identity—not in the opinions of others, but in who God says you are. You are loved, chosen, and valuable in God's eyes.

Action: Regularly affirm your identity in Christ by speaking Scriptures over your life that remind you of God's unconditional love and purpose for you (Ephesians 2:10, 1 Peter 2:9).

9. Living in Freedom and Joy- As healing progresses, you will begin to feel the freedom that comes from releasing the past and embracing the future. Joy and peace return as God mends the broken pieces of your heart. This freedom allows you to live in the present without the burden of past wounds holding you back.

Action: Celebrate small victories on your healing journey. Find joy in the present moment, and trust that God is restoring your heart in ways beyond your expectations.

10. Walking in Purpose - Healing is not the end of the journey—it is a new beginning. Often, the pain you've overcome becomes the very thing that equips you to help others. Walking in your purpose means using your story of healing to encourage and uplift those who may be struggling.

Action: Pray for God to reveal how your journey can inspire or support others. Serve in ministries, volunteer, or mentor others who are walking a similar path of healing.

The road to freedom and true healing is paved with grace, perseverance, and a willingness to surrender the brokenness to God. Healing doesn't happen overnight, but with each step, the heart, mind, and soul are restored by God's love. Through this process, you will find peace, joy, and the freedom to live a life no longer defined by past hurts, but by the abundance and purpose God has for you.

A Prayer for Healing and Freedom After a Divorce

Heavenly Father,

I come before You today with a heart that is heavy and weary. The journey I have walked through—the pain of divorce, the loss, the brokenness—it weighs deeply on me. Yet, even in the midst of this heartache, I know that You are with me. You are the God who sees, the God who hears, and the God who heals. In my brokenness, I turn to You, trusting that You are my refuge and strength, a very present help in times of trouble (Psalm 46:1).

Lord, this season of life has not been easy. Divorce feels like a tearing of the heart and soul. It is more than just a legal process; it is the unraveling of dreams, the shattering of promises, and the loss of a future once imagined. The pain runs deep, Lord, and there are days when it feels like I might not make it through. But You, O God, are the healer of broken hearts. Your Word tells me that You are close to the brokenhearted and that You save those who are crushed in spirit (Psalm 34:18). So today, Father, I ask that You draw near to me in this time of deep sorrow and grief.

Lord, I bring my pain to You. I lay before You every hurt, every wound, and every tear that I have cried in this season. The loneliness, the rejection, the feelings of failure—they are all too much for me to carry on my own. But You, Lord, invite me to cast all my burdens upon You because You care for me (1 Peter 5:7). So, I lay it all down at Your feet, trusting that You will take the weight of this pain and carry it for me. I ask for Your comfort, Lord. I need Your peace to cover me, to quiet the storms within my heart, and to remind me that I am not alone. You are with me, even in the midst of this painful chapter of my life.

Father, I ask for healing. Divorce leaves deep wounds—wounds that often take time to heal. But I know that You are the Great Physician, and there is no wound too deep for You to heal. I ask that You touch the places in my heart that are broken and restore them with Your love and grace. Heal the wounds of betrayal, rejection, and disappointment. Heal the pain of separation and the loss of what once was. I invite You into every broken place, trusting that You will bring healing in Your perfect way and in Your perfect time.

I pray also for healing in my mind. Divorce can leave behind so many thoughts that weigh heavily—thoughts of guilt, shame, regret, and self-doubt. Lord, I ask that You renew my mind with Your truth. Remind me that I am not defined by this divorce. I am not a failure. I am not unworthy. I am not unlovable. I am Your child, deeply loved, redeemed, and restored. I ask that You silence the lies of the enemy that try to convince me otherwise. Fill my mind with Your truth, Lord, and let that truth set me free (John 8:32).

Lord, I ask for freedom. I don't want to carry the weight of this divorce with me for the rest of my life. I don't want to live in the past, replaying what went wrong, blaming myself or others, or being bound by bitterness and resentment. I want to be free, Lord—free to move forward into the life You have for me, free to embrace the new beginnings You are offering, and free to walk in the fullness of Your joy and peace. Your Word says that where the Spirit of the Lord is, there is freedom (2 Corinthians 3:17), and so I invite Your Spirit to work in me, setting me free from the chains of the past and leading me into the freedom that only You can give.

Help me to forgive, Lord. I know that forgiveness is part of the healing process, and yet it can be so hard to forgive when the pain is still fresh. But I also know that holding onto unforgiveness only keeps me bound in chains of bitterness. So today, Lord, I choose to forgive. I forgive my ex-spouse for the pain they caused me, for the promises that were broken, and for the hurtful words and actions. I release them into Your hands, trusting that You are the ultimate Judge and that You will deal with all things in Your perfect justice. I also ask for Your help in forgiving myself. Divorce can leave behind so much self-blame and regret, but I know that I am not perfect, and neither is anyone else. I choose to release myself from the weight of guilt, trusting that Your grace is sufficient to cover my mistakes.

Father, I ask for new beginnings. This chapter of my life may be ending, but I believe that You are a God of new beginnings. Your Word says that You are doing a new thing, and that You make a way in the wilderness and streams in the wasteland (Isaiah 43:19). So, I ask that You guide me into the new things You have prepared for me. Lead me into new opportunities, new relationships, and new paths that are in line with Your will for my life. Help me to trust that even though this part of my journey has been painful, you are working all things together for my good (Romans 8:28).

I ask for the courage to embrace the unknown. Divorce can leave me feeling uncertain about the future—unsure of what's next or how to move forward. But I trust that You hold my future in Your hands, and that You have good plans for me—plans to give me hope and a future (Jeremiah 29:11). Help me to walk forward in faith, trusting that You are with me every step of the way. Let me not be afraid of the unknown, but instead let me be excited about the new possibilities that lie ahead. I trust that You are leading me into a new season of freedom, healing, and restoration

Lord, I also ask for the strength to rebuild. Divorce can leave behind broken pieces, and it can feel overwhelming to think about rebuilding my life after such a painful experience. But I know that You are a God who rebuilds and restores. Just as You restored Job's life after he went through great loss, I trust that You will restore mine as well. Help me to take one step at a time, relying on Your strength and not my own. Let me rebuild my life on the solid foundation of Your Word and Your love, knowing that You are the One who will establish my steps and direct my path.

Father, I pray for joy to return to my life. Divorce can steal so much—peace, hope, and especially joy. But I believe that You are the giver of joy, and that joy is not dependent on my circumstances. Your Word says that You turn mourning into dancing and that You give beauty for ashes (Isaiah 61:3). So, I ask that You restore my joy, Lord. Let me find joy in Your presence, for in Your presence there is fullness of joy (Psalm 16:11). Let joy rise up in my heart once again, even in the midst of this difficult season. Let it be a joy that is unshakable, a joy that is rooted in the knowledge that I am loved by You and that You are working all things for my good.

Lord, I thank You for Your faithfulness. Even in the midst of this painful season, I see Your hand at work in my life. You have never left me, and You never will. You have walked with me through the darkest moments, and You continue to guide me into the light. I thank You for Your love, Your grace, and Your mercy. I thank You for the ways You are healing me, restoring me, and setting me free. And I thank You for the new beginnings that are ahead.

Father, I commit myself to You fully. I surrender my heart, my mind, my body, and my soul to You. I trust that You are in control, and I place my future in Your hands. Let Your will be done in my life and let everything I do be for Your glory. I am Yours, Lord, and I trust that You will lead me into a place of healing, freedom, and peace.

In Jesus' name, I pray.

Amen.

Chapter Nineteen
P.T.S.D (Powerful, Triumphant, Saved, Devoted)

The story (my story) of a young woman who rises from the ashes of heartbreak, abuse, rape, and divorce to find healing, strength, and triumph through faith is one of remarkable resilience. Life can often seem like a series of insurmountable challenges, but for those who persevere, who refuse to let the brokenness define them, there is beauty beyond the pain. This chapter takes you inside a transformative journey of a woman who, once broken and shattered, discovered her power and ultimately her true self through the grace of God. Her story illustrates how pain can give birth to purpose, and how faith can serve as the cornerstone for not only survival but a life of joy and fulfillment. Heartbreak, abuse, and rape are not just words; they are experiences that crush the soul, leaving a young woman feeling powerless and deeply wounded. For our protagonist, her journey began in the dark valleys of these traumas, where she was left emotionally and spiritually devastated. She trusted those who betrayed her, endured unimaginable abuse, and suffered from the scars of rape that made her feel violated beyond repair.

Divorce added yet another layer of grief, pulling the last semblance of security from under her. She had married young, believing in the promise of love, but the marriage was riddled with toxicity, manipulation, and emotional violence. When it ended, it felt like the final nail in the coffin of her self-worth. She saw herself as a broken vessel, unworthy of love, and undeserving of happiness. Her soul was tired, and the weight of shame and guilt pressed upon her heart like a heavy stone. Yet, in deepest valley, something within her refused to give up entirely. There was a faint flicker of hope, a whisper that perhaps this was not the end of her story. This whisper came not from the world, but from God—whose voice she was yet to fully recognize. Healing is never instantaneous.

It is a journey that involves reliving the pain, acknowledging the scars, and confronting the broken pieces of one's soul. For this young woman, the turning point came when she realized that, despite everything she had endured, there was still power within her. Her circumstances did not define her. God did. And God's definition of her was far greater than her self-perception. Through prayer, therapy, and the support of a faith community, she began to rediscover the strength she had buried deep within herself. Each day, she fought to overcome the haunting memories, the shame of her past, and the lies that had been spoken over her. She learned to see herself not as a victim, but as a survivor. More importantly, she learned to forgive—not just those who had hurt her, but herself. Forgiveness became her pathway to freedom, a way to unchain herself from the bitterness that threatened to consume her.

Through her faith, she began to see herself through God's eyes: loved, valued, and powerful. The same God who had walked with her through the valley of despair was now leading her toward victory. She meditated on scriptures that reminded her of her worth—Psalm 139:14 became her anthem, reminding her that she was "fearfully and wonderfully made." Slowly, but surely, she began to reclaim her identity and her voice. As she healed, something remarkable happened: her life began to flourish. Where once there was despair, there was now hope. Where there was brokenness, there was now restoration. Her relationship with God deepened, and she found a new sense of purpose in helping others who had endured similar pain. She became a beacon of light for those still walking through their valleys, using her story to bring comfort and encouragement to the broken-hearted.

God had not only healed her wounds; He had given her a platform to inspire others. She returned to school, completed her education, and even started a non-profit organization dedicated to supporting women who had experienced trauma. Her life, once marked by darkness, now radiated with the joy of the Lord. She found fulfillment not in the validation of others, but in the purpose, God had for her. She no longer needed to seek love from external sources—she had found the greatest love of all in her relationship with God.

This woman, once broken, had become triumphant. The abuse and pain that once threatened to destroy her became the foundation upon which her new life was built. She had been through the fire, and she came out not as ash, but as gold—refined and shining brighter than ever before. Perhaps the greatest victory in her story was not found in her external achievements, but in her internal peace. For the first time, she experienced true joy. Her heart, once fractured by heartbreak and trauma, was whole again. She had learned that happiness was not dependent on circumstances or relationships but was rooted in the unshakable love of God.

She devoted her life to serving others, recognizing that her healing was not meant for herself alone, but for the countless others who needed hope. Through her ministry, she shared her testimony with women from all walks of life, reminding them that they too could rise from the ashes. Her life became a living testimony to the transformative power of faith, hope, and love. In the end, this young woman (ME) had not only found herself in God—she had found freedom. She had discovered the strength to live a life unburdened by her past, a life where she was no longer defined by what had happened to her, but by the love of the One who had saved her. The journey from brokenness to triumph is never easy, but it is always possible through faith and perseverance.
It's a pleasure to share my story because my story reminds us that no matter how deep the wounds, healing is possible, and a life of joy and purpose can be found on the other side of pain. In finding my true self in God, I discovered that my scars did not diminish me—they only made me stronger. My story is not just one of survival, but of triumph, a testimony to the power of faith, and the unending love of God that transforms even the most broken into the most beautiful.

A Prayer for Triumphant, Salvation, and Devotion

Heavenly Father,

I come before You with a heart full of gratitude, love, and awe for all that You have done in my life. You are the God of my salvation, the One who has rescued me from darkness and brought me into the light of Your glorious presence. You have taken me from the pit of despair and lifted me into the fullness of Your grace and mercy. I worship You, Lord, and I declare Your goodness over every part of my life. You have made me triumphant, saved by Your precious blood, and now I stand here as a devoted follower of Christ, fully surrendered to Your will.
Lord, I thank You for the triumph You have given me. There have been battles, valleys, and storms in my life, but through it all, you have made me victorious. I did not overcome by my own strength, but by Your Spirit and by Your power. You are the One who fights for me, and with You, I know that I can never fail. Your Word reminds me that we are more than conquerors through Christ who loves us (Romans 8:37). Even when I faced overwhelming circumstances, you gave me the strength to stand firm. Even when I felt weak and defeated, you gave me courage and filled me with hope. You have delivered me from every trap, every attack, and every fear that sought to destroy me. Lord, I declare today that I am triumphant, not because of anything I have done, but because of who You are and the victory You won on the cross.
Father, I recognize that my triumph is rooted in the salvation You have given me. I was lost, but now I am found. I was dead in my sins, but You have made me alive in Christ. I am saved, not by my works, but by Your grace. How can I ever thank You enough for the gift of salvation? You saw me in my brokenness, in my rebellion, in my sin, and You chose to save me. You sent Your Son, Jesus, to die on the cross for my sins, to take my place and bear the punishment that I deserved. And because of His sacrifice, I am forgiven, cleansed, and made new. I am no longer defined by my past mistakes or failures. I am a new creation in Christ (2 Corinthians 5:17), and I stand here today, saved and redeemed by Your love.
Thank You, Lord, for the assurance of salvation. Your Word tells me

that nothing can separate me from Your love, not death, nor life, nor angels, nor demons, nor anything else in all of creation (Romans 8:38-39). I am secure in Your hands, and I know that my salvation is eternal. Even when I fall short, even when I struggle, you are faithful to me. Your mercy is new every morning, and Your grace is always sufficient for me. Lord, I rejoice in the fact that I am saved by Your grace, and I will forever praise You for the incredible gift of salvation that You have given me.

Father, as one who is saved, I commit myself to being fully devoted to You. You are my Lord and my Savior, and I want to live a life that reflects my love for You. I do not want to be half-hearted or lukewarm in my devotion to You. I want to give You everything—my heart, my mind, my soul, and my strength. I want to live a life of complete surrender, where every part of me belongs to You and is used for Your glory

Lord, help me to be devoted to You in every area of my life. In my thoughts, let me meditate on Your Word Day and night, so that my mind is constantly focused on Your truth. Let my heart be filled with love for You, so that everything I do flows from a place of deep affection and devotion. In my actions, let me serve You with excellence, seeking to glorify You in all that I do. Whether I am at work, at home, or in ministry, let everything I do be an offering of worship to You.

Father, I ask that You strengthen my devotion to You in my prayer life. Prayer is the lifeline that connects me to You, and I want to be faithful in spending time in Your presence. Help me to pray without ceasing (1 Thessalonians 5:17), bringing every concern, every joy, and every need before You. Let me not just come to You with my requests, but with a heart that desires to know You more deeply. I want to hear Your voice, to experience Your presence, and to be transformed by the time I spend with You in prayer. Draw me closer to You, Lord, as I commit to a life of devoted prayer and communion with You.

Lord, I also ask that You deepen my devotion to Your Word. Your Word is a lamp to my feet and a light to my path (Psalm 119:105). It is the source of wisdom, guidance, and truth. I want to be someone who delights in Your Word, who meditates on it day and night, and who allows it to shape my heart and my life. Help me to study Your Word diligently, to understand it deeply, and to apply it faithfully. Let Your Word dwell in me richly, so that I am transformed by its power and truth.

Father, I ask for the grace to be devoted to You in my relationships.

Let the love You have poured into my heart overflow to those around me. Help me to love others as You have loved me, to serve others as You have served me, and to forgive others as You have forgiven me. Let my devotion to You be evident in the way I treat others—in my kindness, my patience, my humility, and my compassion. Let me reflect Your love in all my interactions, so that others may see Christ in me and be drawn to You.

Lord, I know that true devotion requires sacrifice. There are times when following You will require me to lay down my own desires, my own plans, and my own comfort. But I am willing, Lord, to take up my cross daily and follow You (Luke 9:23). I trust that whatever I give up for You, you will replace with something far greater. Help me to live with an eternal perspective, knowing that the things of this world are temporary, but the things of Your kingdom are eternal. Let my heart be fully devoted to You, willing to surrender whatever is necessary in order to follow You more closely.

Father, I ask that my devotion to You would grow stronger with each passing day. Let my love for You deepen as I experience more of Your goodness, grace, and faithfulness. Let my faith in You grow as I see Your hand at work in my life. Let my commitment to serving You become even more resolute, as I walk in the purpose You have for me. I want to live a life that honors You in every way, and I ask that You continue to mold me and shape me into the person You have called me to be.

Lord, I declare today that I am triumphant, saved, and devoted. I stand in the victory that You have given me, knowing that I am more than a conqueror through Christ. I rejoice in the salvation You have provided, knowing that I am redeemed, forgiven, and secure in Your love. And I commit myself to a life of complete devotion to You, knowing that there is no greater joy than living for Your glory.

Father, I thank You for the journey that has brought me to this place of triumph, salvation, and devotion. It has not always been easy, but through every trial, every challenge, and every victory, you have been faithful. You have never left me, and You never will. I know that the road ahead will still have its challenges, but I am confident that You will continue to lead me, guide me, and strengthen me every step of the way I offer myself to You, Lord, as a living sacrifice, holy and pleasing to You. This is my spiritual act of worship (Romans 12:1), and I ask that You would be glorified in my life from this day forward and forevermore.

In Jesus' mighty name, I pray,

Amen.

Chapter Twenty
Evolution

What is it like to evolve? Have you ever imagined the process of a butterfly? A butterfly starts as a caterpillar who later enters a cocoon. The cocoon is dark and unpleasant, however, once the cocoon breaks a beautiful butterfly appears. The butterfly is now free from bondage, from the darkness that once surrounded it, and is ready to explore what the world has to offer. The core meaning of what it truly means to evolve is the gradual development of something more complex, being able to evolve through our daily choices. As I began to journey through life, I began to evolve into the young lady that I was destined to become.

Stepping into a new era of my life has never been easy for me, nonetheless, it is a part. of my journey. Traveling through our teenage years are moments when we are free to explore and enjoy life. Well for me my journey was hard and often difficult to handle at times. I was never the most popular girl in school, I always felt like an outcast. Many of my friends were very few and often I traveled through life not knowing what to do. Although I wanted to be liked and loved, I hid behind a smile. A smile that often spoke the truth while other times a smile that spoke joy, happiness, and triumph.

This was the moment where depression became my appetizer, bullying became my breakfast, self-doubt became my lunch, and low self-esteem became my dinner. While facing obstacles on every end I was on the verge of a mental breakdown. Suffering the loss of grandparents who meant the world to me an absent father who abandoned me, the death of my aunt, and my mother, and moving through the obstacles of a broken marriage, and now the turmoil that lies within has truly begun to take an effect on me. While walking the path called life there were many times when I felt all alone. On many occasions, I often wondered what my purpose in life was and why did God leave me there. God became a person whom I hardly spoke of anymore because the relationship I once had with the creator had been tainted by the illusion of what he was supposed to be versus who he was.

As an outcast, it became difficult to trust people because of hidden motives that rested within them. It was almost impossible to find a friend who would love me for who I was. I was a shy young lady but often well-spoken at times, I was timid but courageous, trustworthy but humble, and talented but anointed. I was not the average woman for I was thin and fragile, innocent, and modest. I was not built like a fashion model nor displayed the body features of the most beautiful woman in my life, yet I wanted to be accepted. The most important person whom I needed was the main one I shut out and that was God. Often, we will turn our backs on God, but God is a man who will never turn his back on us because no matter what we do, he is always there with open arms ready to receive us back into his loving arms. I was walking through darkness because my physical eyes were closed to what God was trying to show me in the spiritual realm. I had to let go and begin to trust God for the plan he had for my life.

Evolving in Christ is a profound journey that encompasses spiritual growth, personal transformation, and deepening one's relationship with God. This process is not merely about following religious practices but involves a continuous, transformative engagement with Christ that shapes every aspect of life. It requires commitment, reflection, and a willingness to align oneself with the teachings and example of Jesus. At the heart of evolving in Christ is cultivating a personal relationship with Him. This relationship is founded on faith and is nurtured through regular communication with God. Prayer is the primary means of this communication, serving as a channel for expressing gratitude, seeking guidance, and confessing struggles. Consistent, heartfelt prayer helps to deepen one's connection with Christ, allowing His presence to become a guiding force in everyday life.

Studying Scripture is another vital aspect of this relationship. The Bible provides the teachings and principles that shape Christian living. Engaging in regular Bible reading and meditation allows believers to understand God's will gain insight into Christ's life and teachings and apply these lessons to their own lives. Reflecting on Scripture in the context of personal experiences can illuminate areas of growth and encourage deeper spiritual understanding. Spiritual discipline involves practices that foster growth and maturity in the Christian faith. These disciplines include prayer, fasting, and service. Each discipline plays a role in shaping one's character and drawing closer to Christ. Engaging in regular, earnest prayer is foundational to spiritual growth. It provides an opportunity to align one's desires with God's will, seek strength for challenges, and express reliance on His grace. Prayer should be both personal and communal, allowing for both individual reflection and shared supplication within the church community.

Fasting is a practice that encourages reliance on God and the prioritization of spiritual nourishment over physical needs. It can be a powerful tool for breaking away from worldly distractions and focusing more intently on God's presence and guidance. Being involved in a church community allows for mutual support and spiritual nurturing. Through communal worship, Bible study, and fellowship, believers can strengthen their faith, gain new perspectives, and find encouragement in their spiritual journeys. Additionally, serving within the community helps to build a sense of belonging and purpose, reinforcing the call to live out one's faith in action. Evolving in Christ is a dynamic and ongoing process that involves deepening one's relationship with Him, practicing spiritual disciplines, embracing moral growth, and engaging in the community. This journey requires dedication, self-reflection, and a willingness to align one's life with the teachings of Jesus. As believers commit to this path, they experience transformation and growth, reflecting the love and grace of Christ in their lives. Through continuous effort and reliance on God's guidance, individuals can evolve in Christ, growing closer to Him and embodying His teachings in their daily lives.

A Prayer for Learning How to Evolve in Christ

Heavenly Father,

In this sacred moment of reflection and devotion, I come before You with a humble heart, seeking Your guidance and grace as I embark on the journey to evolve in Christ. Lord, I recognize that evolving in Christ is a profound process that demands transformation, growth, and a deepening of my relationship with You. I ask for Your divine wisdom and strength to navigate this path with faithfulness and dedication. I pray for Your wisdom to illuminate my understanding of Your Word and Your will for my life. As I seek to grow closer to You, grant me the insight to grasp the teachings of Scripture and the discernment to apply these lessons to my daily life. Help me to approach Your Word with an open heart and a willing spirit, eager to learn and be transformed by Your truth. May Your Holy Spirit guide me in my study and reflection, enabling me to grow in knowledge and love for You.
Teach me the art of prayer, so that I might engage in sincere and meaningful conversations with You. Help me cultivate a habit of prayer that is both personal and communal, allowing me to express my deepest concerns, joys, and gratitude. I seek Your guidance in developing a prayer life that nurtures my spiritual growth and draws me closer to You. Grant me the discipline to pray regularly, the humility to seek Your guidance, and the trust to rely on Your grace in every aspect of my life. In my journey towards evolving in Christ, I acknowledge my weaknesses and areas of growth. I pray for Your healing touch to mend the brokenness within me and to help me overcome the obstacles that hinder my spiritual progress. Strengthen me to face challenges with courage and resilience, and comfort me in times of struggle. Let Your grace be sufficient for my needs, and Your love be a constant reminder of Your presence and support. Heal my heart from past wounds and guide me towards a future of wholeness and renewal. Guide me in practicing spiritual disciplines that foster my growth and transformation in Christ. Help me to develop a routine of daily Scripture reading, meditation, and reflection that deepens my relationship with You. Teach me the value of fasting and how it can draw me closer to Your will. Inspire me to serve others with a heart full of compassion,

reflecting Christ's love through my actions. Let these disciplines become a natural and joyful part of my life, shaping me into a vessel of Your grace and truth.

Instill in me a heart of love and forgiveness, following the example of Christ. Help me to love others unconditionally, as You have loved me. Teach me to extend grace and compassion, even when it is difficult, and to forgive those who have wronged me. Let my actions reflect Christ's teachings and be a testament to Your transformative power. Empower me to build bridges of reconciliation and to live out the call to love my neighbor as myself. In my pursuit of spiritual growth, surround me with a supportive community that encourages and strengthens my faith. Lead me to a church family where I can find fellowship, accountability, and mutual support. Help me to engage actively in the life of the church, participating in worship, study, and service. May the relationships I build within the Christian community be sources of encouragement and growth, helping me to remain steadfast in my journey toward becoming more like Christ. As I seek to evolve in Christ, I trust in Your power to transform and renew me. Help me to embrace the changes that come with spiritual growth, even when they are challenging or uncomfortable. Let Your Spirit work within me to produce the fruit of the Spirit such as love, joy, peace, patience, kindness, goodness, faithfulness, gentleness, and self-control. Transform my mind, heart, and actions to align with Your will, and let my life reflect Your grace and truth. Grant me a clear vision of the purpose You have for my life as I seek to evolve in Christ. Help me to understand and embrace the unique calling You have placed on my life, using my gifts and talents to serve others and advance Your Kingdom. Inspire me to pursue a life that is aligned with Your purposes, and to live with intentionality and passion in all that I do. Let my journey of faith be marked by a deep sense of purpose and a commitment to living out Your will. I thank You for Your unfailing love and the promise of Your presence as I strive to evolve in Christ. I place my trust in Your guidance, knowing that You will lead me through this journey with grace and truth. Strengthen me in my commitment to follow Christ, and help me to grow in faith, hope, and love. May my life reflect Your goodness and a testament to Your transformative power.

In Jesus Name

Amen.

Chapter Twenty-One
Finding My Way

In a world often characterized by its rapid pace and complex challenges, many individuals find themselves drifting away from spiritual practices and religious beliefs that once provided comfort and guidance. This journey back to faith, however, is not only possible but can be profoundly transformative. Reconnecting with God involves introspection, understanding, and practical steps that reflect a sincere desire to reestablish one's spiritual path. This book explores the process of finding your way back to God, focusing on understanding the disconnect, practical steps for reconnection, and the transformative effects of renewed faith.

To begin the journey back to God, it is essential first to understand why the disconnect occurred. There are numerous reasons why individuals may feel estranged from their faith. Life events, such as personal trauma, loss, or significant changes, can challenge one's belief system. Additionally, societal influences and shifting priorities may contribute to a diminished focus on spiritual practices. Often, a period of doubt or skepticism can grow into a more pronounced estrangement if not addressed. Identifying the root causes of this disconnect is crucial. For some, it may be a matter of unanswered questions or perceived contradictions within religious teachings. Others might struggle with feelings of inadequacy or guilt, believing they have drifted too far to return. Recognizing these underlying issues is the first step in the process of reconnection.

The journey back to God often begins with a period of self-reflection. An honest examination of one's spiritual beliefs, practices, and the reasons behind the disconnect can provide clarity. Journaling or meditation can be helpful tools in this process, allowing individuals to explore their thoughts and feelings about faith without judgment. Reconnecting with faith often involves seeking guidance from others. This could include reaching out to spiritual leaders, mentors, or members of a faith community. Engaging in discussions with others who have navigated similar journeys can provide valuable insights and encouragement. Reemerging oneself in religious texts and practices is a fundamental step in rekindling one's faith. Reading scripture, participating in prayer, and engaging in other spiritual disciplines can foster a deeper understanding of and connection to one's beliefs. It is important to approach these practices with an open heart and mind, allowing for personal growth and renewal.

Being part of a faith community can offer support and accountability. Attending religious services, joining study groups, or participating in community service can help rebuild a sense of belonging and purpose. The shared experience of faith can encourage and reinforce one's commitment. The journey back to God is also an opportunity for personal transformation. Embracing forgiveness, letting go of past grievances, and committing to a lifestyle that reflects one's beliefs can lead to profound changes in one's outlook and behavior. This transformation is often accompanied by a renewed sense of peace and purpose.

The process of finding your way back to God can lead to significant personal and spiritual transformation. Many individuals report a renewed sense of inner peace, clarity, and purpose as they reestablish their connection with God. This renewed faith often brings about a deeper understanding of oneself and one's place in the world. Furthermore, reestablishing one's faith can lead to stronger relationships with others. A renewed commitment to spiritual values often results in a greater sense of compassion, empathy, and understanding in one's interactions. This can improve relationships with family, friends, and the broader community.

In addition, the process of reconnecting with God can also provide a sense of direction and resilience. With faith as a guiding force, individuals often find themselves better equipped to navigate life's challenges and uncertainties. The comfort and strength derived from spiritual beliefs can be a source of support during difficult times. Finding my way back to God became a deeply personal journey that involved understanding the reasons for the disconnect, taking practical steps toward reconnection, and experiencing the transformative effects of renewed faith. While the path has been challenging, it offers the possibility of profound personal and spiritual growth.

By engaging in self-reflection, seeking guidance, immersing myself in spiritual practices, participating in community, and embracing personal transformation, I was able to rediscover a sense of purpose, peace, and connection. Ultimately, this journey is not just about returning to a set of beliefs, but about finding a deeper and more meaningful relationship with the divine.

A Prayer for Direction & Guidance

Heavenly Father,

In Your presence, I seek solace and understanding. You are the source of all wisdom and knowledge, the guiding light in times of darkness. I come to You today, humbled and seeking Your divine direction for my life. In a world full of choices and uncertainties, I ask for Your guidance to lead me on the path that You have ordained for me. Lord, I acknowledge that I am, but a vessel and it is Your will that I wish to follow. My heart is open to Your voice, and I pray that You speak clearly to me. Help me to discern Your will in every decision I face. Whether it's a choice about my career, relationships, or personal growth, let Your wisdom illuminate my path.

Grant me the patience to wait for Your timing and the faith to trust in Your plans. Sometimes, the way forward is not immediately clear, and I feel lost and unsure. In these moments, remind me of Your promises and your steadfast love. Strengthen my faith so that I may find peace in knowing that You are in control and that Your plans are always for my good. Guide me, O Lord, with Your gentle hand. When I am faced with decisions, big or small, let Your voice be louder than any other. May I not be swayed by fleeting desires or external pressures, but instead remain steadfast in seeking Your will. Teach me to recognize Your guidance in the stillness and to follow it with courage and conviction. Father, grant me discernment to see beyond my immediate desires and to understand the broader picture of Your plans for me. Help me to make decisions that are not only beneficial to myself but also serve to further Your kingdom and bring glory to Your name. Let my choices reflect Your love and grace, and may they be in alignment with Your divine purpose.

In times of doubt and confusion, be my anchor and my guide. When the path seems unclear, remind me of Your faithfulness and Your promise to never leave nor forsake me. Let Your peace guard my heart and mind as I navigate through the complexities of life. Help me to trust in Your wisdom, even when I cannot see the way ahead.

Lord, I also ask for the strength to accept Your guidance, even when it leads me away from my plans and desires. Teach me to let go of my agenda and embrace the path You have set before me. Help me to trust that Your ways are higher than mine and that Your plans are always for my good.

Grant me the humility to seek counsel and the wisdom to recognize Your voice in the advice of others. Surround me with individuals who reflect Your truth and who can provide guidance and support in alignment with Your will. Let their words and actions reflect Your love and wisdom. Father, I pray for clarity in moments of indecision. Let Your word be a lamp to my feet and a light to my path. As I immerse myself in Scripture and prayer, may I find guidance and encouragement that direct my steps according to Your will? Help me to be diligent in seeking Your guidance through Your word and prayer.

In every aspect of my life, I seek Your direction. Whether it's in my professional endeavors, my relationships, or my personal growth, let Your will be done. Help me to approach each situation with a heart open to Your leadership and a spirit willing to follow Your direction. As I walk this journey, remind me that I am never alone.

Your presence goes before me, and Your hand guides me. Help me to trust in Your timing and to remain steadfast in faith, knowing that You are orchestrating every detail of my life for Your glory and my good. Lord, I place my future in Your hands, confident that You are leading me according to Your perfect plan. Help me to remain faithful in my walk with You, to seek Your guidance with an open heart, and to follow Your direction with unwavering trust.

Thank You, Father, for Your constant guidance and for the assurance that You are with me every step of the way. May I always seek You first and trust in Your divine plan for my life.

In the name of Jesus Christ, I pray, Amen.

Chapter Twenty- Two
Her Name is ME

Understanding who God says you are as a woman involves exploring various biblical teachings and principles that highlight the unique value, purpose, and identity of women in God's eyes. The Bible affirms the dignity, strength, and significance of women, offering a powerful foundation for understanding your identity as a woman of God. Are you going through an emotional time in your life where you think God had taken his hands off you? Are you at the point of no return and you feel like God is silent? Have you cried endless tears and needed a word from God? Have you fallen completely on your face crying out to the Master and in return your prayers and calls went unanswered?
Have you ever longed for love only to receive hurt? Did you reach out for someone's hand only in return for becoming abused by the same hands who said they will never hurt you? Have you ever given your heart to someone only to have it handed back to you shattered into pieces?

Have you ever wanted something or someone so bad to where it almost cost you a life? Possibly your very own life? Often, we cry and beg for things that we know is not healthy for us. God will give us what we want only in return to show us it's not what we really need. When we learn how to take our hands out of the cookie jar, then and only then when we will be able to see what God has in store for us.
Learning to love yourself and forgiveness are the most key factors you must possess in this life. Although I was kind, gentle, loving, displayed a heart of gold, smart, intelligent, and just a ray of sunshine, I did not love myself. The betrayal from someone I called family and loved like a brother, the pain from bad relationships, and the anger built up -I lost my identity, I lost who I was, I lost all hope, and my thrill was gone. One Sunday morning, God shined upon his love and the Holy Spirit led me to a place that has now became my haven-Rehoboth International Ministries and Grace Baptist.

God has so many things in store for me and he has so many things in store for you as well. If you have experienced a life like I have, I want you to know your breakthrough is on the way. I want you to understand your next level of overflow begins with you opening your mouth and giving him what he deserves. If we can praise and worship him during our hurt, pain, suffering, disappointment, and anger you will be surprised to see the overflow he shines upon our life when you praise him through the joyous times. God is never silent, and he never sleeps. God hears those silent tears, and it is him who rocks you to sleep in those lonely hours. God loves you, for he created you in his image. You are his daughter and his son for you belong to him. God came to give life and give it more abundantly. What makes him so special is GOD does not treat us as our sins deserve.

God is a man who look past all our faults, and he see the good in us. God is a way maker, miracle worker, comforter, king of king, restorer, healer, deliverer, and he is our provider. It does not matter how low you are because his loves flow to the lowest valley. I once read where author Bobby Stapleton, once said broken pieces still swim. It doesn't matter how broken you are God can still mend those broken pieces and he can still use you for the kingdom of God. God is the only one who can make you whole again. The author continues in his writing by saying, your lifeguard walks on water. God will reach down and pull you up when you are sinking. God will never let you sink. Understanding who God says you are as a woman or as a man involves exploring various biblical teachings and principles that highlight the unique value, purpose, and identity of women in God's eyes. The Bible affirms the dignity, strength, and significance of women, offering a powerful foundation for understanding your identity as a man or woman of God. Being created in God's image means that you reflect His character, creativity, and capacity for love and relationship.

Your identity is rooted in this divine image, which gives you intrinsic value and purpose beyond societal expectations or roles. Embrace your identity as a reflection of God, recognizing that your worth is not determined by external factors but by your Creator. This understanding empowers you to live with confidence and purpose, knowing that you are valued and loved by God. Galatians 3:28 declares, "There is neither Jew nor Gentile, neither slave nor free, nor is there male and female, for you are all one in Christ Jesus." This verse affirms the equal value of men and women in the eyes of God and within the body of Christ. You must never let the ways of the world deter you of who God has called you to be. You must never allow the enemy to trick you into thinking you are not good enough. You are who God say you are. You are the daughter and son of a king, you are beautiful, you are radiant, you are kind, you are a gentle spirit, and you are on your way to the next level in your life. We can all learn from my experience because the enemy tried to slay me, but God had purpose for my life.

A Prayer for Loving Who God Has Called Me to Be

Heavenly Father,

I come before You with a heart overflowing with gratitude. As I reflect on who You have called me to be, I am in awe of Your love, grace, and the divine purpose You have instilled in me. Thank You, Lord, for Your constant presence in my life, for guiding me, shaping me, and calling me according to Your perfect will. Lord, I thank You for creating me in Your image. You are the Master Creator, and I am humbled that You have formed me with such care and intention. As it says in Psalm 139:13-14, "For You created my inmost being You knit me together in my mother's womb. I praise You because I am fearfully and wonderfully made; Your works are wonderful; I know that full well." Thank You, Father, for the unique identity You have given me. You designed every part of me with purpose, and I am grateful that I reflect Your image. Help me to always remember that my value comes from being Your creation, not from the opinions or standards of this world.

Thank You for the gifts, talents, and abilities You have placed within me. I recognize that these are not for my glory but for Yours. May I use them to serve others and to bring honor to Your name. I am grateful for the opportunities You have provided for me to grow and develop these gifts, and I ask that You continue to guide me as I seek to fulfill the purpose for which You created me. Father, I am overwhelmed by the depth of Your love for me. Your love is unconditional, steadfast, and never-ending. Even when I have strayed from Your path, you have always been there, calling me back to You with open arms. Your grace has covered my sins, and Your mercy has lifted me up when I have fallen. I thank You for loving me not because of what I have done, but because of who You are.

Thank You, Lord, for adopting me as Your child. In Ephesians 1:4-5, Your Word says, "For He chose us in Him before the creation of the world to be holy and blameless in His sight. In love He predestined us for adoption to sonship through Jesus Christ, in accordance with His pleasure and will." I am so grateful that You chose me, that You have called me to be part of Your family. Your love gives me a sense of belonging, security, and identity. I am not defined by the world, but by Your love for me. Thank You for Your grace that is sufficient for me, even in my weakness. I am grateful that Your power is made perfect in my weakness (2 Corinthians 12:9). When I feel inadequate or unworthy, your grace reassures me that I am enough because You are enough. I thank You for the strength You provide to overcome challenges and to live out the calling You have placed on my life.

Lord, I thank You for the unique calling You have placed on my life. You have called me by name and have a purpose for me that is far greater than I could ever imagine. Jeremiah 29:11 reminds me that Your plans for me are to prosper me and not to harm me, to give me hope and a future. I am grateful that You guide my steps and direct my path, even when I do not see the full picture. You are the Good Shepherd who leads me beside still waters and restores my soul. Thank You for the ways You have led me through valleys and mountains, always keeping me close to Your heart.

Thank You for equipping me with the gifts, talents, and abilities needed to fulfill the purpose You have for me. You have not left me to figure it out on my own but have provided everything I need through the power of Your Holy Spirit. I am grateful for the opportunities You have given me to serve, to love, and to make a difference in the lives of others. Thank You for the people You have placed in my life who have encouraged, supported, and walked alongside me in this journey of faith

Lord, as I close this prayer, I want to once again express my deep gratitude for all that You have done in my life. Thank You for creating me, loving me, calling me, strengthening me, valuing me, and redeeming me. I am who I am because of You, and I am so grateful for the identity You have given me in Christ. May I live each day in a way that honors You and reflects Your love to the world. I commit myself to Your will and ask for Your guidance as I continue to grow in my understanding of who You have called me to be.

In Jesus' name, I pray, Amen.

Chapter Twenty- Three
My Testimony

Life's journey is often marked by trials and tribulations that test the very core of our being. For a young woman, whose life has been marred by hurt, pain, betrayal, rape, domestic violence, and suffering, these experiences could have easily led to a life of despair. However, my story is not one of defeat but of triumph. Through the grace of Christ, I found a way to transcend the darkness and emerge into His divine glory, using my experiences to inspire and uplift others. This book explores my journey, the challenges I've faced, and how I transformed my suffering into a powerful testament of faith and resilience. Betrayal by loved ones and friends is perhaps one of the most profound forms of hurt a person can experience. It shakes the foundation of trust and leaves scars that can take years to heal. For me as a young woman, betrayal was not just a momentary lapse in judgment by those I trusted; it was a recurring theme that shaped much of my early life. Friends who turned their backs on me in times of need, loved ones who inflicted emotional wounds, and the overwhelming sense of abandonment all contributed to a deep sense of isolation.

The pain I endured was compounded by the physical and emotional trauma of rape and domestic violence. These experiences left me feeling violated, powerless, and unworthy of love. The scars of such trauma run deep, affecting not only the body but also the soul. The weight of these experiences could have easily led me down a path of self-destruction, but even in the darkest moments, there was a flicker of hope that kept me going. The cumulative effect of betrayal, abuse, and suffering can lead to a place of darkness, where hope seems like a distant memory. For me as a young woman, the darkness was not just a metaphorical concept; it was a reality I lived every day. The feelings of worthlessness, shame, and guilt were overwhelming, leading me to a state of stagnation where it seemed impossible to move forward. The world around me felt like a hostile place, filled with reminders of the pain I had endured.

In this dark place, I grappled with questions of purpose and identity.

Who was I beyond the pain? Could I ever escape the shadow of my past? The answers were not immediately apparent, and the journey to finding them was fraught with obstacles. Yet even as I teetered on the edge of despair, there was a part of me that refused to give up. The turning point in my life came when I found my way to Christ. It was not an immediate or easy transformation, but rather a gradual awakening to the presence of a higher power that had been guiding me all along. Through prayer, meditation, and a deepening relationship with Christ, I began to see my experiences in a new light.

Christ offered me something that the world could not—a sense of unconditional love and acceptance. In Him, I found solace for my wounded soul and a refuge from the storms of life. Through His teachings, I learned that my suffering was not in vain, but rather a part of a larger plan to bring me closer to His divine purpose. As I delved deeper into my faith, I began to understand that Christ had been with me in every moment of my suffering, offering me strength even when I felt weak. This realization was both humbling and empowering, as it allowed me to let go of the shame and guilt that had plagued me for so long. I began to see myself not as a victim, but as a survivor, and more importantly, as a child of God.

With Christ as my guide, I embarked on a journey of healing and transformation. This was not a linear process, but one marked by setbacks and challenges. However, each step forward brought me closer to the light, and each obstacle I overcame strengthened my faith. One of the most significant aspects of my healing was the process of forgiveness. Through Christ, I learned the importance of forgiving those who had wronged me, not for their sake, but for my own. Forgiveness was the key to releasing the hold that pain and bitterness had on my heart. It allowed me to break free from the chains of my past and step into a future filled with possibility.

In addition to forgiveness, I also found healing in sharing my story on many platforms. Writing became a form of therapy, a way to process my emotions and make sense of my experiences. Through my writing, I was able to give voice to the pain I had endured, but more importantly, I was able to share the hope and redemption I found in Christ. My words became a beacon of light for others who were going through similar struggles, offering them the same hope that had sustained me. As I continued to walk in faith, I began to experience a profound transformation. No longer was I defined by my past; instead, I was becoming a new creation in Christ. The darkness that had once consumed me was replaced by the radiant light of His love, and I began to see myself through His eyes as a beloved daughter, cherished and valued.

This evolution was not just spiritual, but also practical. I began to set new goals for my life, ones that were aligned with my divine purpose. I pursued her passions with renewed vigor, using my talents and gifts to glorify God. My writing, once a means of survival, became a ministry through which I could reach others and share the message of hope and healing. In this new season of my life, I experienced a sense of joy and peace that I had never known before. The burdens of my past were lifted, and I was free to walk in the fullness of God's plan for my life.

My story became a testament to the transformative power of Christ's love a reminder that no matter how deep the darkness, His light can always break through. The journey of such an amazing woman is one of incredible resilience and faith. Through Christ, I was able to overcome the hurt, pain, betrayal, and suffering that once defined my life. My story is a powerful reminder that even in the darkest of circumstances, there is always hope. With Christ as my anchor, I was able to evolve from a place of stagnation into a life filled with purpose and divine glory. My life is a testament to the truth that with God, all things are possible, and that no matter how deep the wounds, His love has the power to heal and transform.

A Prayer of Overcoming I am a Living Testimony

Divine God,

I come before You today with a heart full of gratitude and awe for the ways You have worked in my life. I stand here as a living testimony of Your faithfulness, Your grace, and Your power. Lord, I am an overcomer—not by my own strength, not by my own wisdom, but by the power of Your Spirit and the testimony You have given me. I declare today that I am victorious, not because of who I am, but because of who You are in my life.

Father, as I reflect on my journey, I am reminded of the countless battles I have faced. There were moments when I thought I couldn't make it, when the weight of life's struggles seemed too heavy to bear. Yet, in those moments, you were there, carrying me, strengthening me, and lifting me up when I was weak. You have proven to be my rock, my refuge, and my deliverer. I am here today because of You, Lord, and I give You all the glory for the victories You have brought me through.

Lord, I thank You for the power of my testimony. Your Word tells me that we overcome by the blood of the Lamb and the word of our testimony (Revelation 12:11). My story is a testament to Your goodness and grace. Every trial, every storm, every hardship I've endured has been part of the testimony that You are writing in my life. Through it all, I have seen Your hand at work, molding me, shaping me, and preparing me for the purpose You have for me.

I remember the times of struggle, Lord. There were seasons when life seemed unbearable—when I felt lost, confused, and broken. I didn't understand why I had to walk through such difficult paths. But looking back, I can see how You used those very moments to strengthen my faith, to deepen my trust in You, and to build a testimony of Your power. What the enemy meant for harm; you have turned for good (Genesis 50:20). You have taken the ashes of my pain and turned them into something beautiful, and I praise You for that, Lord.

Father, I thank You for the battles I have won in Your name. There were addictions I couldn't break, but You broke them. There were fears that paralyzed me, but You delivered me. There were strongholds that had me bound, but You set me free. Every victory I have experienced is because of Your grace, and I am forever grateful. You have made me more than a conqueror through Christ who loves me (Romans 8:37). Lord, I realize that the power of my testimony lies in more than just my words—it is in the transformation You have brought in my life. I am not who I used to be. I am no longer defined by my past, by my failures, or by the mistakes I've made. I am a new creation in Christ (2 Corinthians 5:17), and I walk in the newness of life that You have given me. I am a living testimony of Your redemption, and I pray that my life will always reflect the victory that You have secured for me on the cross.

Father, I thank You for the strength to overcome. There were moments when I felt like giving up, when the weight of life's trials seemed too much to bear. But in those moments, you reminded me that Your strength is made perfect in my weakness (2 Corinthians 12:9). It was not by my own power or might that I overcame, but by Your Spirit. You have been my source of strength when I was weary, my comfort when I was hurting, and my guide when I was lost. I am victorious because You have been my constant help. Lord, I acknowledge that my testimony is not just for me—it is for others. There are people who need to hear my story, who need to know that the same God who brought me through the fire can bring them through as well. I pray, Father, that You would use my testimony to encourage others, to bring hope to those who are struggling, and to point them to You. Let my life be a living testament to Your goodness and grace, and may my testimony inspire others to trust in You and seek Your face.

Lord, I thank You for the future victories You have in store for me. I know that the journey is not over, and that there will be more challenges ahead. But I face the future with confidence, knowing that You are with me and that You have already given me the victory. Your Word tells me that You have overcome the world, and because of that, I can walk in victory no matter what I face (John 16:33).

Father, I pray that You would continue to strengthen me as I walk this journey of faith.

Help me to remain steadfast in the face of adversity, to trust You even when I don't understand, and to lean on Your strength when I am weak. I know that there will be more battles to fight, but I also know that You are the One who fights for me, and with You on my side, I cannot be defeated. I declare today that I am an overcomer by the blood of the Lamb and by the word of my testimony. Lord, I also pray

for those who are going through their own battles right now. There are so many people who are struggling—who feel like they can't make it, who are weighed down by the cares of this world. I pray, Father, that You would give them the strength to keep going, the faith to trust in You, and the courage to believe that they, too, can overcome. Use my testimony as a source of encouragement for them, Lord. Let them see that if You could bring me through, you can do the same for them. Let my life be a living testament to Your faithfulness and Your power.
Father, I commit my testimony to You. I thank You for every battle I have faced, every victory You have given me, and every lesson You have taught me along the way. I know that my story is not finished, and I trust that You are still writing it. I ask that You continue to use my testimony for Your glory. Let it be a beacon of hope to those who are lost, a source of strength to those who are weary, and a reminder to all that You are a God who saves, who delivers, and who makes us overcomers. I declare today, Lord, that I am an overcomer by Your grace. I am victorious, not because of anything I have done, but because of what You have done for me. I will continue to walk in the power of my testimony, trusting in Your faithfulness and Your love. I will share my story with others, knowing that it is not just my story—it is a story of Your goodness, Your mercy, and Your grace.
Lord, I thank You for the power of testimony. It reminds me of where I have been and where You have brought me. It is a constant reminder that You are a God who never fails, who never abandons Your children, and who always leads us to victory. I am grateful for the testimony You have given me, and I pray that it would always bring glory to Your name.

In Jesus' mighty name, I pray,
Amen.

How to Stay Grounded and Faithful in Christ: A Path to Divine Acceleration

Staying grounded in Christ while seeking divine acceleration involves balancing a deep spiritual connection with an active pursuit of your God-given purpose. Here are key steps to help you remain anchored in your faith while experiencing divine acceleration:

1. Prioritize Daily Communion with God
To stay grounded, maintaining a strong relationship with God through prayer and meditation is vital. Prioritize personal time with Him to connect, seek guidance, and listen for His voice.

"But seek first the kingdom of God and His righteousness, and all these things will be added to you." — Matthew 6:33

Practical Steps: Set aside quiet time daily for prayer, scripture reading, and reflection. This builds your spiritual foundation, reminding you that acceleration without Christ is empty.

2. Immerse Yourself in the Word of God
God's Word is the anchor of our faith and provides direction for divine acceleration. The Bible will remind you of God's promises and show you His ways, helping you stay focused on what truly matters.

"Your word is a lamp to my feet and a light to my path." — Psalm 119:105

Practical Steps: Memorize key scriptures, meditate on God's promises, and allow His Word to shape your decisions. The Word becomes a roadmap that guides you in moments of challenge or uncertainty.

3. Stay Humble and Obedient to God's Leading
Humility is essential for staying grounded in Christ. Acknowledge that all success and acceleration come from Him. In moments of elevation, remember to remain humble and obedient to His direction.

"Humble yourselves, therefore, under God's mighty hand, that He may lift you up in due time." — 1 Peter 5:6

Practical Steps: Keep an attitude of gratitude and service. Even in times of success, ask God for the grace to walk humbly and serve others as Christ did.

4. Surround Yourself with a Godly Community
Staying grounded requires being surrounded by others who share your faith. Fellowship with believers will keep you accountable and encourage you during seasons of both acceleration and challenge.

"As iron sharpens iron, so one person sharpens another." — Proverbs 27:17

Practical Steps: Join a church community, participate in Bible study groups, or develop close relationships with people who will pray for and uplift you. This support will keep you steady as God accelerates your growth.

5. Cultivate a Lifestyle of Worship and Praise
Worship is one of the best ways to stay connected to Christ, especially during seasons of acceleration. When your heart is filled with gratitude and awe for God, you remain focused on Him and His power rather than your own.

"Let everything that has breath praise the Lord. Praise the Lord." — Psalm 150:6

Practical Steps: Spend time praising God daily, whether through song, words of adoration, or acts of thanksgiving. Worship places you in a posture of surrender, reminding you that God is the source of all progress.

6. Trust God's Timing and Process
Divine acceleration doesn't mean skipping the process. Often, God accelerates us through seasons of waiting or difficulty to refine our character and deepen our dependence on Him. Trusting in God's timing ensures that your foundation remains solid.

"There is a time for everything, and a season for every activity under the heavens." — Ecclesiastes 3:1

Practical Steps: Be patient in the process and trust that God is preparing you for the acceleration He has in store. Avoid the temptation to rush or take shortcuts, knowing that His plans are perfect.

7. Walk in Faith, Not Fear
Divine acceleration requires stepping out in faith and trusting God with your future. Stay grounded by believing in His promises and rejecting fear. Fear causes us to lose sight of Christ, while faith propels us forward.

"For God has not given us a spirit of fear, but of power and of love and of a sound mind." — 2 Timothy 1:7

Practical Steps: Whenever fear arises, declare God's promises over your life. Affirm your faith in His ability to lead and accelerate you toward His purpose.

8. Maintain a Spirit of Generosity
Staying grounded in Christ means recognizing that your blessings and acceleration are meant to bless others. Live generously, sharing your time, resources, and talents with those around you.

"Give, and it will be given to you. A good measure, pressed down, shaken together and running over, will be poured into your lap." — Luke 6:38

Practical Steps: Practice giving and serving others, even as you experience acceleration. This will keep your heart aligned with God's love and remind you that divine acceleration isn't just for personal gain.

Remaining grounded in Christ during seasons of divine acceleration is about building your life on His principles, trusting His timing, and continually seeking His presence. As you stay rooted in Him, He will guide you through every phase of acceleration with wisdom, peace, and purpose. Let God be your foundation, your anchor, and your guide as He accelerates you into the next season of your life. Stay close to Him, and you will find that divine acceleration is not about rushing, but about growing deeper in your walk with Christ while fulfilling His purpose for your life.

"Wait for the Lord; be strong, and let your heart take courage; wait for the Lord!" — Psalm 27:14

This simple but powerful declaration speaks to the essence of faith. When life feels overwhelming, and the future seems uncertain, waiting on God is an act of trust that He is working behind the scenes. His timing is perfect, and in those moments of waiting, He renews our strength and deepens our belief in His promises.
This powerful statement encourages us to trust in God's timing, even when life feels uncertain or overwhelming. In moments of waiting, we often struggle with doubt, fear, or impatience, but God's Word reminds us that waiting on Him is never in vain. He is always working behind the scenes, orchestrating circumstances for our good, even when we can't see it. Believing in this truth allows us to release our worries and rest in His promises.

Waiting on God is not a passive act but an intentional decision to place our trust in His plans. As we wait, God strengthens us, giving us the courage to face whatever challenges come our way. It is in this period of waiting that our faith is refined, and we grow in spiritual maturity. Instead of relying on our own strength, we learn to lean on His, knowing that He will renew our hope and give us the endurance to persevere. Belief is the key to unlocking the strength God provides. When we choose to believe in His goodness and faithfulness, even when circumstances are difficult, we open ourselves up to experience His peace and strength in a deeper way. By simply trusting in His plan, we allow God to work in our lives, building resilience and preparing us for the blessings He has in store. In the end, waiting on God brings forth a strength and joy that can only come from fully surrendering to Him.

A Message from the Author Never Stop Believing in Yourself and in God

Dear Reader,

I want to take this moment to remind you of something deeply important—never stop believing in yourself, and more importantly, never stop believing in God. Life has a way of testing our faith and challenging our sense of purpose. There will be times when the road ahead seems uncertain, when you may feel lost, or even question whether the dreams you hold so dearly will ever come true. But let me assure you, there is a plan for your life that is greater than anything you could ever imagine, and it is authored by God Himself.

Even when life doesn't make sense, you must trust that God is working things out for your good. His ways are higher than ours, and often, His plan doesn't unfold in the way we expect. Yet, that does not mean He has abandoned us or forgotten the dreams He planted in our hearts. Trusting in God's timing is crucial, even when the wait seems endless. Remember, some of the greatest blessings in life come through seasons of waiting, struggle, and uncertainty. These moments are designed not to break you but to mold you into the person God created you to be.

God's plan for you is beyond anything you can comprehend. The path may not always be easy, but you have been given all the strength you need to walk it. He knows every detail of your life—every hurt, every triumph, every tear, and every smile. He is not only the Creator of the universe but also the One who cares intimately about the smallest details of your journey. Trust in His love, in His power, and in His promise that nothing is too hard for Him. He can do the impossible in your life, and with Him by your side, you can accomplish what you once thought was unattainable.

As you navigate through life, never stop dreaming. Hold fast to the dreams that God has placed within you because those dreams are seeds, He planted for a purpose. They are the vision of what He knows you can achieve. I know it can be tempting to let go of a dream when the road is long, and the obstacles seem overwhelming. But remember, the size of the dream God gave you reflects the greatness He has placed within you. You are not walking this journey alone—He is with you, guiding every step, opening doors, and closing others to protect you from paths that were never meant for you.

There is no dream too big for the God we serve. He is a God of the impossible. If He has placed a vision or dream in your heart, He has also equipped you with everything you need to see it come to pass. You may not have all the answers right now, but trust that God is at work, even in ways you cannot see. When things seem uncertain, when fear creeps in, remind yourself that God is the author of your story, and He has already written the victory.

Finally, let me encourage you to be kind to yourself along the way. We are often our own worst critics, doubting our worth and our ability to reach the heights we aspire to. But know this—you are fearfully and wonderfully made, a masterpiece in the hands of the Creator. He sees your potential even when you cannot. Believe in yourself, not just because of your own abilities, but because of the One who created you for greatness.

So, keep going. Keep dreaming. Keep believing. God is with you, and He is faithful to complete the good work He has started in you. Your dreams are not out of reach—they are just waiting for you to step into the fullness of the destiny God has prepared for you. With God, nothing is impossible. He is the God of limitless possibilities, and as you trust Him and believe in yourself, you will see that all things are truly possible for those who believe.

With love and faith,

Cathy L. Benson

MEET THE AUTHOR

Cathy L. Benson, a remarkable author hailing from Pearl, Mississippi, and now residing in Riverdale, Georgia. Cathy's journey with writing began as a simple hobby in her youth, but over time, it blossomed into her greatest passion. As a devoted mother of two daughters—one who is currently serving in the Navy (Aasia Arieyelle) and the other a high school sophomore (Zion Faith)—Cathy has balanced her personal life with a deep commitment to serving others. She dedicates her days to caring for veterans, embodying a spirit of service and gratitude for the country she loves.

What truly defines Cathy is her unwavering faith in God, which has guided her through every chapter of her life. Her story is one of transformation—turning pain into purpose, trauma into triumph, and stagnation into acceleration. Cathy's testimony speaks to the power of resilience and faith, as she has allowed God to shape her into a divine vessel for the Kingdom. Through her writing, she aims to inspire others to embrace their own journeys of healing, growth, and spiritual awakening.

Cathy L. Benson is a beacon of strength, and her life's work reflects her dedication not only to her craft but also to the people she serves and the God she follows. Her writing, infused with her personal experiences and faith, stands as a testament to the power of transformation, showing that through God's guidance, struggles can indeed lead to success.

Made in the USA
Columbia, SC
05 June 2025

59003701R00080